A BOND THAT BREAKS

JOSH WINSCHEL
AND
TERRI BROWN

Fulton Books, Inc.
Meadville, PA

Published by Fulton Books 2021

Disclaimer: This book is completely fiction. All references to actual names and places are used creatively.

ISBN 978-1-64952-221-4 (paperback)
ISBN 978-1-64952-222-1 (digital)

Printed in the United States of America

CHARACTER RELATIONSHIP

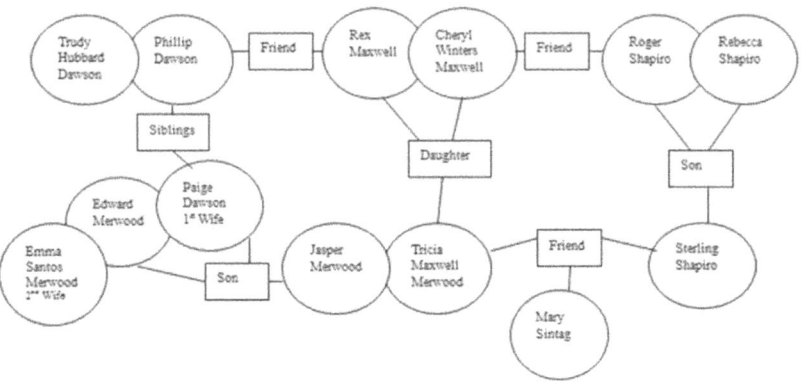

PART 1

CHAPTER 1

December 21, 2018, 6:00 PM

Ring. Voice mail. Tricia's phone is still shut off.

Jasper Merwood stood among the hordes on the subway platform in the early evening hours of this the last Friday before Christmas. The crowd was quite merry. And in the spirit of the season, they were uncharacteristically patient, polite, and even friendly. They were responding positively to the ringing bells at the Salvation Army buckets and generously giving to the poor, homeless souls bundled up within the subway halls and staircases. Many carried packages in various stages of wrap, some the spoils of office-party grab bags, and others set to be gifted at romantic dinners or under beautifully decorated trees. They were humming along with Bing Crosby to the familiar lyrics of "White Christmas" as it played over the subway speakers.

Jasper too had spent the afternoon with colleagues, exchanging gifts, drinking cocktails, and congratulating each other on the conclusion of a very successful year at Paxton Goldberg, a prestigious investment firm on Wall Street and a division of the Merwood Real Estate and Investment Corporation. Jasper had recently inherited the company from his father. Despite all this joy and gaiety surrounding him, Jasper was not in the Christmas spirit. His life for the last four months had been one calamity after another, and he was beginning to feel like Job from the Old Testament.

Jasper looked at the screen that hung from the ceiling at the platform. He saw that a Queens express was due to roar through the terminal without stopping in less than a minute. The Green Line crosstown to Manhattan was racing right behind it. This would be Jasper's train, and he, in addition to many others, pushed forward in anticipation. As Jasper noted the thunderous sound of the express about to race by, he felt a force on his upper back. The jostling sent Jasper off the edge of the platform, and as he screamed out, an observant man on his left placed a strong hand on his jacket collar, pulling Jasper back to safety.

"Whoa there, fella, are you okay?" asked the man.

Jasper was in shock but instinctively said, "Thank you. I believe you just saved my life."

At 6'2" and 215 pounds, Jasper was strong and quite capable of holding his own. But somehow, at that moment, he felt weak. He had only sipped four vodka tonics during the three-hour office party. *Could I really be that tipsy?*

He looked around at all the passengers surrounding him on the platform. Many were already on their phones texting, Instagramming, and snapping to all they knew about the near tragedy they had just witnessed.

Jasper began to regain his nerves and asked no one in particular, "Did you see what happened? Was I pushed?"

Many shook their heads negatively. Others just shrugged their shoulders and went back to focusing on their phones.

"I think you were just the victim of an overzealous crowd that wants to get home and start celebrating with family," said Jasper's new hero standing beside him. Jasper nodded in agreement as he adjusted his coat one more time.

The Green Line arrived a moment later, and Jasper was fortunate to find a seat. As it had almost every minute of the last week, his mind immediately went to his wife. He and Tricia had tied the knot earlier this year, but now he wasn't sure where she was and she wasn't even answering her phone. While the two of them had experienced some issues lately, Jasper could not accept that Tricia would leave him. Jasper looked at the text message screen on his cell phone for the hundredth time that day. No new messages. *Tricia, where are you?*

At that moment, a headline on the newspaper strewn at Jasper's feet caught his eye. Across the front page, he read, *Private Investigator Mary Sintag Provides Tip that Brings Central Park Killer to Justice.*

Mary Sintag had been a friend of Tricia and Jasper's at the University of Pennsylvania, and she remained close to Tricia to this day. She left school before graduation and entered the police academy. After a few years of foot patrol on Long Island, she retired from the force and started her own PI business. *Maybe Tricia had reached out to Mary?* Jasper decided to give Mary a call.

CHAPTER 2

Jasper

Jasper Merwood grew up in a wealthy suburb of Atlanta, Georgia, the only child of the famed real estate mogul, Edward Merwood, and the beautiful Hollywood actress, Paige Dawson. Jasper lived in a lap of financial luxury. His was a world of servants and excess, a silver spoon in his mouth. However, despite all the money and the latest new age toys and gadgets, Jasper was a lonely child.

He attended school online at one of the most elite virtual academies in the South. Education was emphasized as his father made it clear that Jasper would need to earn his wealth and status; it would not be handed to him.

Edward was a distant father, preferring to spend his time at the condo in Manhattan or the beach house in Key West. Business always took precedence over family. Even after Paige died of a drug overdose at a movie premiere in Cleveland when Jasper was just ten years old, Edward made no attempt to increase his time with Jasper. Looking back, Jasper would have to conclude his best friends growing up were Sophia, the hired chef who doubled as his nanny, and Barney, a shaggy wheaten terrier. Jasper's mother had arranged the delivery of the eight-week-old puppy for his fifth birthday while she was away in Pamplona, Spain, filming the romantic drama, *Final Desire.*

Though Jasper had adapted to the years of solitude, at the age of seventeen, he was looking forward to his adventure at Columbia University, away from the Merwood Estate. Unfortunately, living on campus of the Ivy League college was not what he expected. He never fully adjusted to this vastly diverse environment despite his best efforts to fit in. His underdeveloped conversational skills made him seem arrogant and unapproachable, which hindered his opportunities to make friends.

Jasper was very intelligent, and lacking a social life, he threw himself into his studies. Although his major was undeclared, academically, he excelled at Columbia, and after a successful year, he transferred to the University of Pennsylvania's prestigious Wharton School of Business where he could focus his studies on finance. It was at Penn in the fall of 2011 that Jasper would make a connection to an individual that would change the course of his life: Sterling "Silver" Shapiro.

CHAPTER 3

Unbreakable Bonds Triumphs

The agricultural town of Westfield, New York, is located on the western side of Chautauqua County. Founded in the early 1800s, Westfield is home to Chautauqua Creek, which is a tributary between Lake Erie and Chautauqua Lake.

Centrally located in Lake Erie's wine country, Mr. Maxwell developed what would grow to be the largest, most successful winery in the region. Upon acquisition, his family had established a homestead and began farming the land for corn. Little by little, orchards of grapes and fields of strawberries were planted. Over the years, they had acquired five hundred acres, and in 1960, Unbreakable Bonds was incorporated, which included the farm and UBB Winery.

Mr. Maxwell had an affinity for horses, and in the mid-1970s, he purchased an American quarter horse mare and an Arabian stud. With the profits from the winery, a twenty-two-stall stable was built, and corrals were fenced along the property. Over the years, he bred, trained, and sold many successful race horses, but his pride was Snow, a majestic pure-white mare.

*****

The 1984 Summer Olympic Games in Los Angeles were the highlight of Cheryl Winters's budding career. She returned home to Westfield with one silver and two gold medals. She had been training at UBB stables since the age of five, and now, fourteen years later, she was their hero. Cheryl was a beautiful young woman with an athletic build and soft, inviting facial features. Her long blond hair fell to her hips when it wasn't pulled back in a tight ponytail. She was stunning. Outgoing, determined, and dedicated to her craft, she was becoming the toast of Westfield, so much so that the entire town turned out to line the streets to welcome their Olympian home.

Her future was bright, and the Maxwells were lucky to have her. And no one felt luckier than Rex Maxwell himself, Mr. Maxwell's only child. Rex had always been drawn to Cheryl's beauty and athleticism, and being nine years her senior, he had watched her grow up at the stables. Their friendship developed over the years, but now into adulthood, he spent his evenings dreaming of riding off together to the lake that bordered the property and making love underneath the beautiful weeping willow trees. Unsure if Cheryl reciprocated these feelings, he finally mustered up the nerve to ask her out. He was thrilled to find that she was equally smitten. It wasn't long before Rex's dreams became his reality, and on the evening of their return from California, he proposed to Cheryl at the quaint Italian restaurant, Fabrizio's, where they had gone on their first date two years earlier.

*****

Almost as excited for Cheryl's success as Rex was Roger Shapiro. Roger maintained the UBB stables and loved the horses like none other. He spent hours feeding, grooming, and walking all the horses on the farm, but he enjoyed a special relationship with the Olympic champion, Snow.

Roger's fortunate ties with the Maxwell family were the result of a childhood friendship with young Rex Maxwell. Rex and Roger met in Mrs. Venturi's kindergarten classroom at the Number 4 Elementary School just outside the city limits of Westfield. The two boys were inseparable and spent the school years together finding mischief in every way imaginable. Roger was a natural with the horses and loved working in the stables with Rex. Roger eventually gained full-time employment at the UBB stables, learning all he could from Rex's father, the beloved Mr. Maxwell.

*****

Rex inherited the family business when his father tragically died in a corn-harvesting accident. At just twenty-eight years old, Rex was now in charge of a multimillion-dollar venture, and his first business decision was an easy one. He would promote Roger to partner and give him responsibility over the stables. Together, their efforts over the next few years made UBB the most profitable farm in the region, with over twenty employees, which would double in peak harvest season. Every year, thousands of guests would make the trip to the winery. With its horse-riding opportunities, rolling hills of well-manicured fields, and mesmerizing Lake Erie sunsets, the Maxwells welcomed guests to Westfield in style.

*****

In the summer of 1985, Rex and Cheryl's wedding was the talk of Western New York. The ceremony was held at the stables, and Snow herself walked the rings down the aisle to the happy couple. Many dignitaries attended, including Olympic athletes, local politicians, and corporate bigwigs. The reception took place at the prestigious Longview Country Club. All the planning and preparation had played out perfectly, and the papers reported the next morning that it was the wedding of the century, and anyone who was lucky enough to attend would never forget the experience.

One of those lucky attendees was Phillip Dawson. He had been the main accountant for UBB since graduating from the University of Buffalo and joining his uncle's firm. He and Rex had also become the closest of friends. They shared similar world views and political beliefs. They were always on the same page and could go on for hours about the inadequacies in farm subsidies or the overstepping of the government on anything from environmental requirements to gun regulation. Eventually, in the summer of 1988, when Phillip decided to settle down and marry longtime girlfriend Trudy Hubbard, he would ask Rex Maxwell to be his best man.

Before Rex could focus on Phillip's wedding, his full attention was centered on the 1988 Summer Olympics in Seoul, South Korea. Westfield sent a large contingent to the other side of the world led by Cheryl, Snow, Rex, Roger Shapiro, and his own new bride, Rebecca. Cheryl and Snow were heavy favorites in every event in which they participated. They didn't disappoint, bringing home gold medals in jumping, eventing, and dressage. The next two weeks were filled with parties, celebrations, indulgences, and excessiveness. The group was on top of the world. Their return home to Westfield was again met with pomp and rejoicing. She was given a ceremonial key to the city. Cheryl and Snow were once again heroes of the community.

*****

The next year or so was hectic for Cheryl and Rex. Cheryl was in demand. She had autograph sessions at malls, restaurants, sporting events, and even the convention center in nearby Buffalo. She had guest appearances on television shows and was even offered a cameo in a Hollywood movie. She made rounds on the late-night talk shows and morning news broadcasts.

While Cheryl was busy with her fame, and Trudy was occupied with the upcoming wedding plans, Rex Maxwell and Phillip Dawson would spend lazy evenings at the local tavern or around the fireplace in the farmhouse den recounting the day, telling stories of childhood exploits, or planning future business adventures. Rex was extremely excited that the famous actress, Paige Dawson, Phillip's sister, had agreed to stay the week of the wedding at the main house at UBB.

When the wedding week finally arrived, the farm grounds were in pristine condition. Autumn of 1990 was beautiful in Western New York. The weather was perfect as the days were bright, cool, and crisp. The colorful foliage was in peak presentation. Word had gotten out to the residents of Westfield that Paige Dawson was staying in town, and once again, UBB and the Maxwell family were media darlings.

Initially, Rex and Cheryl were a little starstruck in Paige's presence, but the three of them quickly became comfortable and enjoyed each other's company. Cheryl, embellishing on her small part playing herself in a recent film, would jokingly refer to herself and Paige as a couple of movie stars and Rex as their entourage. Roger and Rebecca Shapiro, for the most part, tried to stay out of the way, but on a couple of evenings, they, along with Phillip and Trudy, joined Paige, Rex, and Cheryl for a night of eating, drinking, gaming, and laughing. Paige mentioned that her husband Edward Merwood had not been around much and appreciated all the companionship from her hosts.

Rex enjoyed showing off the grounds to Paige. She marveled at Snow's beauty and enjoyed watching Cheryl practice their Olympic routine. For all the attention Paige was used to getting as an actress, there was something to be said about the peacefulness of sampling last season's wines while relaxing in the overstuffed leather chairs in the winery's tasting room with Rex. Despite having never met before, their conversations were effortless.

The week was wonderful for everyone and culminated with a beautiful wedding that surpassed Trudy and Phillip's expectations. Rex and Cheryl had been the perfect hosts.

*****

The following spring, Cheryl and Rex learned they were expecting. They were overjoyed. December 22, 1991, a full six days after her due date, Patricia Gertrude Maxwell was born. The elated new parents marveled at the precious little girl.

No doubt this was the peak of happiness for Cheryl. The timing was perfect. She had six months to lose the baby weight and get back in the saddle, literally. The 1992 games in Spain would be the third and final Olympic performance for Cheryl and seventeen-year-old Snow. Despite Rex's objection to another Olympic run, Cheryl insisted and continued to focus on training with Snow. All the while, she remained a dedicated, attentive, and loving mother to sweet little Tricia.

But like most things that reach great heights, soon, they come crashing down, and tragedies would strike the Maxwells and Shapiros in rapid succession.

CHAPTER 4

Unbreakable Bonds, Tragedies

One early morning in April 1992, just three short months before departing for Spain, as she did most days, Cheryl donned her riding uniform and headed to the stables for an intense training session with Snow. Roger Shapiro was already at the stables and had the white mare saddled.

It was a beautiful spring morning. The birds were chirping, the trees were starting to bud, and the daffodils and tulips were in full bloom in the gardens that lined the main house. Walking along the pebbled path to the stables, Cheryl didn't notice the renewing beauty all around her; her thoughts were focused on mounting Snow and getting in a good Olympic training workout.

As Cheryl approached, Roger greeted her with a hearty, "Good morning, Cheryl. Snow is ready to work." Then turning to the magnificent creature, he patted her head and said, "Aren't you, girl?"

Cheryl responded with a distracted nod, barely acknowledging Roger as she took the reins and led Snow out to the corral B behind the guesthouse.

Roger had been working on the side of the barn closest to the corral where Cheryl was practicing when he suddenly heard several loud shrieks. He ran toward the screams and was traumatized by what he saw. Both Cheryl and Snow were on the ground. Snow had misjudged a water gate, landed awkwardly, and thrown Cheryl into an adjacent brick wall obstacle. Roger helped Cheryl to a nearby bench and called for stable hands to come quickly and tend to Snow. Chaos ensued. At first, Cheryl refused to leave Snow, but the pain in her shoulder, neck, and back was too much for her to bear. An ambulance rushed her to nearby Westfield Memorial Hospital. Cheryl broke her collarbone and was fitted with a neck brace and arm sling. Snow suffered an irreparable broken leg.

The two-time Olympian mare had to be put down. Cheryl was the one to administer the fatal injection of sodium pentobarbital.

*****

Three months after that accident, another devastating blow was struck upon the Maxwells. Very suddenly and unexpectedly, the heretofore healthy, strong, and athletic Rex Maxwell suffered a heart attack and died just shortly after his thirty-sixth birthday. No one understood how this possibly could have happened. Rex must have died of an undetectable heart defect or just an unfortunate blip in his system, they reasoned. In any case, Cheryl had hit rock bottom; she began to act erratically. She battled depression and spent long periods alone in her room. She begged out of most social situations and was on a constant emotional roller coaster, quick to lash out in anger one moment, then break down in tears the next. Rebecca Shapiro took a leave of absence as manager of the winery to help Cheryl care for the now eight-month-old Tricia.

Roger, although deeply saddened over the loss of Snow and even more affected by losing his best friend Rex, took over running UBB with unparalleled efficiency. His love for the horses was as strong as it had ever been. Despite Cheryl's absence in helping to run the business, the stables and winery continued to thrive.

*****

Roger and Rebecca Shapiro had a love that was so genuine and pure that it would bring joy to all who saw it. How wonderfully happy they were when they learned Rebecca was expecting a child of their own. They spent every free minute preparing the nursery in the guesthouse on the UBB land they called home. Finally, the big day arrived.

On August 14, 1993, Rebecca went into labor with Roger by her side at Westfield Memorial Hospital. Two people couldn't have been more excited to bring life into this world. But a little more than an hour into labor, machines started beeping, and nurses and doctors began rushing around, racing equipment into the room, and ushering a startled and terrified Roger out. Thirty-five minutes later, Sterling Shapiro entered this world. And five minutes after that, Rebecca left it.

Roger was inconsolable. His perfect life and his perfect future were gone, destroyed in a flash. While the staff of UBB kept everything running, Roger became a shell of his former self.

Roger's calamity had the opposite effect on Cheryl, breaking her from her own desolation from losing Snow and Rex. She had loved UBB before she was even a Maxwell, and she was not about to lose it. Not only did she have her almost two-year-old daughter to care for, but she also took on the role of raising Sterling, doting on him as if her own. Cheryl felt a renewed responsibility; only *she* was in control of her future.

While Roger took time off to heal, Cheryl took over the reins and resumed governing the entities of Unbreakable Bonds. Business boomed, and with her giving riding lessons again, UBB stables produced two of the country's top equestrian athletes of the millennium's last decade. Roger slowly became more involved again in the business aspects of the stables.

Yes, the Maxwells and Shapiros had suffered greatly, but they had rebounded.

CHAPTER 5

December 21, 2018, 9:00 PM

Jasper arrived first and was seated at a table in the rear of the poorly lit Dim Sum Palace. He ordered two beers. While Tricia had remained close to Mary, Jasper suddenly realized he had not seen her in over five years. He couldn't believe it had been so long. Mary had been invited to Jasper and Tricia's wedding, but a lead on a case she was working broke that morning, and her plans were aborted.

Jasper had just gotten settled and taken a big refreshing gulp of his tall draft when Mary walked through the door. At first, his view of her was skewed by a woman in a NY Jets tassel cap walking in his direction. But as the woman turned to head to the ladies' room, the familiar face of the attractive, blonde-haired would-be blind date all those years ago was staring back at him. Jasper rose, and the two embraced warmly.

"Now, there's a sight for sore eyes. Hello, Mary," Jasper said.

"It is nice to see you too, Jammers," replied Mary as Jasper handed her a beer, and they took their seats.

"I have thought about you often over the last few months. I am so sorry about the loss of your father and stepmother. I can only imagine what you are feeling and how difficult these holidays must be."

"Thanks, Mary. Four months ago, I was on such a high. It feels like four years ago now," Jasper said, letting out a long sigh. After a moment, he added, "It almost all ended earlier tonight...," Jasper relayed the near miss in the subway. "I can't get rid of the feeling I was pushed."

"Oh my god, Jasper! What do you mean 'pushed'? Like someone accidently bumped into you?"

"No. As in someone intentionally tried to push me in front of the Queens express."

"But why would anyone want to harm you?" Mary asked quizzically.

"I don't know, Mary. I just don't know. But right now, we need to focus on Trish."

"Okay, Jasper, I'll let it go for now." Mary shifted in her seat. "You said on the phone that you haven't heard from her since she left for her mother's Wednesday morning."

"Yes. It's just not like her. I mean, I know I have been difficult to live with the last couple of months. With Dad dying and me taking over Paxton Goldberg, I've been quite ill-tempered and short-fused, and I have unduly taken that out on Trish. But she wouldn't leave me...and certainly not without warning," Jasper explained emphatically.

"So she didn't suggest she was unhappy?"

"She did. She complained that I wasn't around...and I haven't been. I bury my sorrows with long days at the office then drown them most nights at Bobby G's. Trish said we needed some quality time. We needed to reignite *us*. We hadn't been out or done much of anything together lately."

"Are you cheating on her, Jammers?" Mary asked in an accusatory voice. "I remember your reputation in college."

"Mary! I love Trish! I am not cheating on my wife!"

A little irritated that Mary would even ask that, Jasper half-heart-edly tapped his mug to hers and said, "Here's to my life." And with that, Jasper swallowed down the rest of his beer.

As if on cue, the waitress brought the next round. For a moment, silence hung between Jasper and Mary, an odd juxtaposition to the festive crowd that had gathered at the popular Chinese hangout on Forty-Sixth Street in Midtown Manhattan. The waitress offered tonight's special, the General Tso's platter, but Jasper and Mary declined.

"You mentioned Bobby G's. So you've been drinking a lot? You never were the most fun drunk, Jammers," Mary said with a judgmental tone, remembering some difficult nights on campus with an unmanageable Jasper. Maybe Tricia just had enough.

"I hear you. But she wouldn't do this... She just wouldn't walk out on me."

The look on Jasper's face convinced Mary this wasn't about Tricia avoiding him. This was a man in a desperate spot, and Mary needed to help him.

"Okay, Jasper. So did Trish tell you why she was leaving?"

"Her mother had called and said she needed help with some things. There was no way I could make it. With all the year-end financial reports due, I couldn't spare the time away from work. In fact, we just closed everything up today."

"But you were invited?" Mary asked, insisting.

Jasper paused in thought. "As a matter of fact, Mary, I wasn't. Mine and Tricia's struggles culminated at Thanksgiving when she planned on us going to UBB, and I told her I wanted to have a quiet celebration at home. She was thrilled with that idea. She planned a traditional full-course meal with all the trimmings, but then I went and ruined it."

Mary looked sullen. "Oh no, Jasper, what did you do?"

"I went out Thanksgiving Eve for one drink and came home four hours later, banged my head on the coffee table, and basically told her to get away from me before I eventually passed out. Believe me, Mary, when Cheryl called and asked Trish to go to the farm, she was all too happy to get away.

"It was perfect timing—except for the fact that tomorrow is her birthday. Anyway, I figured she would call Wednesday to let me know she arrived safely. She didn't. I called yesterday morning, but her phone was shut off. I sent texts throughout the day, no response. Finally, I called Cheryl yesterday afternoon."

"Good idea. And?" interjected Mary.

"Cheryl told me that they got into a fight, and eventually, she convinced Tricia that it was time to come home and work things out. She also said that Tricia was in no hurry, and she had no idea when I should expect her," Jasper replied.

"So she needed convincing?"

"Yeah, and apparently, a lot of it. In any case, Cheryl was not happy with me, and the call ended quickly."

Mary stated the obvious. "Clearly, she didn't come straight home, nor do we know why she was there in the first place."

Mary's words missed Jasper's ears. After pausing long enough to take another gulp of his beer, very matter-of-factly, Jasper continued, "I was hopeful she would be home by evening, but she never showed."

Jasper stared at the cocktail napkin on the table that had soaked up the condensation of the pilsner.

Mary saw Jasper's pain. "Have you heard from anyone else?"

"I haven't heard from Cheryl since yesterday afternoon's conversation. Sterling hasn't responded to my calls or texts. I even called her boss at the *New York Times*, and he's heard nothing other than Tricia calling Wednesday morning saying she was taking a few days off.

"Mary, Trish isn't at the farm. She isn't home with me. When I call, her phone goes straight to voice mail. Something is wrong. It doesn't take two days to get home to Manhattan from upstate New York. We need to find her."

Mary listened intently to the details Jasper was providing. She too had called and texted Trish after Jasper contacted her earlier and got no response. "Okay, Jammers," Mary said with a smile that she hoped would give her friend optimism. "I agree that Tricia would not just walk away from you. We will go to UBB tomorrow to retrace her steps. We will find her."

Jasper found comfort in Mary's determination and agreed to the trip. He plopped a twenty-dollar bill on the table to cover the bar tab, and as Mary was putting on her coat, she turned to Jasper and asked, "So how is Sterling?"

CHAPTER 6

Sterling "Silver" Shapiro

As far as Sterling was concerned, Cheryl Maxwell was his mother, and Tricia was his sister. It's not that the truth was kept from him. As soon as he was old enough to understand, Roger told Sterling how his mother had died in childbirth. He made sure that Sterling understood it was not his fault and that he should never feel guilty. But too many times, he witnessed his father struggle with painful memories, and he couldn't help but feel responsible for this grief.

Sterling grew up hearing beautiful stories of how happy his mother and father were and how excited Rebecca was to become a mother. Listening to the love in his father's voice when speaking of her, describing her laughter, her sense of humor, and her beauty, Sterling grew up with a deep appreciation for the mother he never met. He was also thankful for Cheryl and the loving environment she created for him. Sterling loved Cheryl as much as she loved him.

Caring for two small children was easier in the main house, and with Roger immersing himself in running UBB to help drown his own sadness, Sterling spent most of his early years with Cheryl and Tricia.

Sterling was an energetic boy. He was adventurous and would spend many days exploring the farthest reaches of the farmlands. He would often leave in the morning and not be seen again until the sun was going down and the dinner bell was ringing. He was extremely athletic, and in junior and senior high school, he was equally adept with a football, a basketball, and a baseball bat. Sterling was rugged and strong, an extremely good-looking young man. He had a natural golden skin tone, and many young women would get lost in his deep dark eyes. At a very young age, a shiny silver streak appeared in his jet-black hair, and the nickname "Silver" was locked in.

Sterling was extremely bright and studious. He performed superbly throughout his schooling. He had the unique ability of being the teacher's pet while still maintaining popular-kid status. Sterling had a very outgoing, jovial personality. He was affable and good-humored. No one disliked Sterling.

Just like his father, Sterling had a passion for the horses and a sense of responsibility for the success of the UBB stables. He respected his father's work ethic and made every effort to emulate it. While Sterling loved his father, he absolutely adored Cheryl. He was obedient to the only mother he knew without fail. He was always striving for her approval and her praise. On the limited occasion when he did something that disappointed her, he felt devastated. Cheryl had even implied numerous times that Sterling would take over UBB one day.

Tricia Maxwell, the birthright heir, was extremely close to Sterling, but she was not too fond of her mother or the workings of Unbreakable Bonds. She had competed for her mother's attention all her life, but for Cheryl, the horses, winery…and Sterling…always came first.

CHAPTER 7

Tricia

Various economic factors began to make it difficult for the partnership of Roger Shapiro and Cheryl Maxwell to maintain financial stability of UBB. While every small town has its share of watering holes frequented by the locals, over the years, the taverns of Westfield NY cohabitated nicely with UBB as the winery business played to a distinctly different customer base. But in the first decade of the twenty-first century, micro brew pubs and craft breweries gained popularity. These upscale chic drinking spots with full menus began to eat into the winery clientele.

The winery was not the only venture to take a hit for the Maxwells; the stable business was struggling too. The further the years got from Cheryl's equestrian heyday, the less name recognition was out there to draw Olympic hopefuls and families with deep pockets to the UBB stables. As a result, the number of horses currently boarded at the stables had dropped to seven from a peak of twenty-two. Half of their best stable hands left for greener pastures, and the maintenance and care for the horses primarily fell to Sterling and Roger.

Lower government subsidies wreaked havoc on the UBB's top-line revenue. Some of the equipment had experienced earlier-than-expected failure, and they had to expedite new machinery purchases ahead of plan. In addition, a couple of bad harvests had the farm business running in the red.

These struggles took their toll on Cheryl and Roger both physically and mentally. Cheryl would often lose focus, and her mind would be in some far-off place. She was forgetful, often failing to pay the bills or order new feed in a timely manner. She even forgot a number of scheduled lessons and would eventually show up unprepared or even disinterested.

In 2008, Roger suffered a mild stroke. This resulted in a partial loss of control of the left side of his body and definitely hindered his ability to maintain the property. Sterling and the farmhands did their best, but business was again failing. Philip Dawson, UBB's accountant, had offered to discuss the possibility of purchasing Unbreakable Bonds and all its holdings with his brother-in-law, Edward Merwood, the successful real estate developer, but Cheryl would not even entertain the proposition.

In August of 2009, over protest from her mother, Tricia committed to leave UBB and head three hours east to Syracuse University. This was not a hard decision for Tricia. She was well aware of the struggles at the farm, and she knew her mother was having a difficult time keeping it all together. But for Tricia, UBB was always a bittersweet place. Growing up without her father and always feeling second place to the horses in her mother's eyes, Tricia was ready to pursue independent ambitions: the S. I. Newhouse School of Public Communications.

As a freshman in high school, Tricia joined the school newspaper, and in her junior year, she became the lead editor. She loved the journalism business. Identifying a story, tracking down leads, interviewing key characters, and especially the writing excited Tricia. She was a fantastic writer; she loved to tell a story. She had the talent and the passion and the dream, and the top journalism school in the nation was just a short drive from home.

While Tricia's relationship with her mother was distant, she was extremely close to Sterling. He supported her decision to follow her dream. He said she would only grow resentful of UBB and her mother if she stayed. Sterling assured Tricia that he would take care of Cheryl and Unbreakable Bonds.

*****

Two years later, Sterling graduated from high school as valedictorian and secured a scholarship to the University of Pennsylvania in Philadelphia in pursuit of a business degree. Cheryl could not have been more proud of him. Sterling said he would use the education to develop contacts and formulate a business plan that would lead Unbreakable Bonds into the future. He made sure his mother knew that he would be there for her the instant she needed something. Just reach out.

Tricia wanted to stay close to Sterling. She found almost all her credits would transfer, so she took the opportunity to transfer to Penn as well. They were both very excited to spend their college years together.

CHAPTER 8

College Years

In classroom 304 of the Franklin D. Roosevelt Lecture Hall, on the well-manicured campus of the reputable Wharton School of Business, Sterling Shapiro met Jasper Merwood. It was the first week of the fall semester of 2011, and the two shared an international finance and currency class that would meet three times a week.

Jasper, the shy introvert that he was, chose a seat in the rear of the classroom. Sterling, arriving late because the line at Dunkin' Donuts was held hostage by a large disheveled gentleman who couldn't decide on jelly or cream-filled, threw himself in the seat next to Jasper. To Jasper's surprise, this coincidental seating arrangement became the start of a lasting friendship.

Over the course of their joint tenure at Penn, Sterling and Jasper found they shared many interests including archery, jazz music, classic films, and hiking the nature trails of the Lehigh Valley. They spent many late nights studying together while drinking their vodka tonics with splashes of lime. The two friends joined a satire book club and loved to debate the pros and cons of big government in a capitalistic environment. They would regularly play paddleball at the University

Racket Center and would compete vigorously with each other in the swim lanes at Cosby Pool.

Sterling was good for Jasper, breaking him from his shell and introducing him to a whole new world of social interaction. A world, it turned out, that suited Jasper well. A world in which he thrived.

Sterling was the type of person that engaged with everyone and who everyone liked to be around. He was jovial and outgoing; a bubbly, extroverted personality that could draw people in and put them at ease. He desired acceptance and craved attention. Sterling would do anything to gain approval. As a result, he mastered the art of adaptive communication, saying what the listener wanted to hear whether the situation required a serious discussion or lighthearted banter.

Jasper, on the other hand, once he gained confidence in the social world, easily commanded respect. He spoke in a fashion that exuded intellectualness. He was insightful and perceptive. His arguments could be logical, based on facts and data, as well as conceptual, containing deep and philosophical theories. While Jasper was clearly the smartest man in the room, he never came off as a braggart. He never spoke down to his audience or treated anyone as inferior. Jasper had a way of melding his awe-inspiring intellect with the pleasant and welcoming tone of his personality. And, unlike Sterling, Jasper did not have to fight to gain anyone's admiration or attention…especially from the ladies.

Jasper had a fondness for voluptuous full-figured blond co-eds and would target these beauties on campus, either approaching them during breaks in his busy class schedule or not-so-randomly running into them at one of the various bars in town. Not until the beginning of his second year at Penn did one of these women make a lasting impression.

It was October 27, 2012, the day of the big Halloween party at Alpha Chi Rho. Jasper had uncharacteristically experienced a bit of a dry spell with the ladies, so Sterling had negotiated to fix him up. Mary Sintag, a feisty freshman in the criminal justice program, had sparkling blue eyes and long blond hair that was only matched in length by her well-toned legs; she was definitely Jasper's type. Sterling had been introduced to Mary through Tricia. After some coaxing about how fun it would be to meet a mystery man in costume, Mary agreed to the blind date with Sterling's best friend.

Jasper and Sterling arrived at the party first. Sterling, standing 5'11" and weighing 190 pounds, decided it would be fun to dress as a horse jockey, with the tight riding boots and helmet with a chin strap. His favorite part of the costume though was the horse whip with which he would antagonize other partygoers. Jasper chose a character from his favorite musical, *Grease*, Danny Zuko. He remembered as a child how Sophia, his nanny, would slick back his hair with gel, and the two would sing and dance along to "*You're the One That I Want.*" He let out a laugh at the memory of Sophia's high-pitched voice singing the "oo oo oo" parts.

When the girls arrived, Sterling bolted out on the front lawn of the fraternity house to greet them. Jasper watched out the bay window with a disposable cup full of cheap beer from one of the many kegs available for tonight's consumption. The blond-haired big-busted beauty Sterling had set him up with was the sexiest police officer he had ever seen. The buttons of her vest were ready to pop, and the heels of her patent leather thigh-high boots added another 4" to her already 5'6" frame. Mary completed the nontraditional police garb look with fishnet stockings and form-fitting short shorts. Jasper was hoping to get frisked by her later.

Just as he was letting his mind wander to using those handcuffs, his eyes glanced behind Mary to the woman giving Sterling a hug. *That must be Tricia*, he thought, almost in disbelief.

Tricia was the opposite of Jasper's type. With shoulder-length dark hair and eyes to match, a petite girl with a well-defined tight facial structure, Tricia was attractive in her own right, but it was not her natural looks that initially drew Jasper in and removed Mary from a night of sultry bliss. It was her costume. Almost like a sign of fate, Tricia was dressed as Rizzo: complete with a short-sleeve fitted shirt cinched at the waist, a pencil-straight tight-as-can-be skirt, and of course, oversized black sunglasses resting on her long, slender nose.

To Mary's disappointment, the night did not go as planned with Jasper as he spent most of the evening in conversation with Tricia. Tricia was confident, brazen, and opinionated. She did not submit to Jasper's charms and challenged him at every turn. Her dry wit and outspoken candor turned Jasper on. And even though it caught him off guard, Jasper was not deterred when Tricia declined the invite to his room that first night; the rejection only furthered his interest.

Jasper and Tricia would see a lot of each other the next few weeks, and both definitely felt an emotional and intellectual attraction. Jasper and Tricia were on their way.

CHAPTER 9

December 22, 2018, 6:30 AM

Ring. Voice mail. Tricia's phone is still shut off.

Jasper was still trying to wake up when he arrived at the small duplex in Queens. Mary lived at 204 East Jackson Street. He spotted John and Jane Andrews, the elderly couple who lived next door to Mary, sitting on the 6' × 6' patio sipping their coffee. The upkeep of the two sides of the property couldn't have been more disparate. For every planter that would house beautiful summer flowers on the Andrewses' side, there was a cardboard box, refuse container, or rusted metal contraption on Mary's side. While the Andrewses' had a stunning freshly painted blue exterior with beige trim shutters, it appeared Mary's half had not seen a paintbrush in many years.

Mary was waiting impatiently and came out immediately when she spotted Jasper's 2019 black Lincoln Continental turning the corner. She was pulling a small suitcase on wheels behind her.

"Nice place," Jasper exclaimed. "Yours is okay too, Mary," he followed with a laugh and a wink in the Andrewses' direction.

"Ha-ha, very funny. Can't keep up with the Andrews. But I know they wish I would try a little harder," grunted Mary. John and Jane raised their cups as if to toast the thought.

"I need to gas up. Let's hit the Sunoco over on Flushing," Jasper said as he tapped the trunk closed.

"Sounds good. I could use some coffee, and let's grab a couple of donuts and some chips," Mary suggested.

Jasper wondered how Mary could maintain such a fit figure while eating all that junk food.

"Perfect. With traffic so light, we should be on Interstate 80 heading west in no time."

Forty-five minutes later, they were enjoying a couple of Long Johns and a rising sun as they left the New York City limits. There wasn't a cloud in the sky, and the weathermen were overly excited to prognosticate near-record temperatures exceeding sixty degrees. For a short while, Mary even had her window down, and the breeze blew her blond locks like a cape behind her as they raced past the barren landscape of leafless trees.

"This weather is amazing," she said.

Jasper agreed. "No doubt about that. Thank goodness it isn't like that trip we took to see Springsteen in Pittsburgh that year at Penn."

"Oh man! What a crazy messed-up trip that was. At least we survived and can look back and laugh."

"For a while, I thought we wouldn't make it. We were stuck on the turnpike for at least six hours surviving on Pringles and Gatorade. You were so mad, Mary, when Sterling finished off the bottle."

"Yeah, but he paid for that! Remember, he had to pee, and as he stepped over the guardrail, the wind blew him face-first into a foot of snow? He was so frustrated," Mary recalled as she slapped her thigh in laughter.

"Trish came up big. She took him up to that Villanova basketball team bus, and he was able to change into a warm-up suit," remembered Jasper. "Tricia has a way with people, that's for sure."

"You and I had so much fun in that car as I recall. You were so funny with all those one-liners. I think I was drunk on laughter."

"Yeah, we had a good time." The corners of Jasper's lips curled up at the memories.

"Jammers," said Mary reflectively, "do you remember our kiss?"

"Of course, I do. How could I forget it? It was Sterling's buddy Max's twenty-first birthday party. I think you and I were the only ones that weren't drunk when we started playing that ridiculous sex game. Thankfully, the card I pulled was just a kiss. Anything more would have become quite awkward," Jasper continued.

"Whose idea was it to play that game anyway?" asked Mary.

"Good ole Max himself." Jasper laughed. "I think that was his gift to himself. I'm glad we bailed when we did."

A little more matter-of-factly, Mary continued, "I remember that kiss. It was nice…very nice." Her voice trailed a bit. "Jammers, do you ever wonder what would have happened if you and I had gotten together that Halloween night as planned?"

Jasper just let the question hang between them. The sign for the rest stop up ahead couldn't have come at a better time. Jasper needed to stretch his legs.

*****

Mary returned to the car carrying coffee and another donut. She put her hand out to Jasper indicating she wanted to drive, and he was more than willing to toss the keys her way. After a long while, lost in their own thoughts, Mary said, "Jammers, I really have thought about you these last few months. I'm sorry I didn't reach out to you when I heard about your dad. I had just seen him on TV the week before in that charity golf tournament at Pebble Beach."

Jasper's mind went back to that September day when he got the news that would start his quick downward slide on the icy slope of tragedy. "It was so unexpected. He was only fifty-three and in great health. In fact, he had just visited his primary care physician for his annual physical, and all his numbers were good. 'Fit as a fiddle' Dad liked to quote the doc."

"I heard about the barbiturates, and I've seen some of the news reports. It sounds like the investigation is going nowhere?" Mary inquired.

"Nowhere fast, Mary." Jasper sighed.

"Well, if his health was good, then it sure does make it sound like foul play."

"He wasn't anxious or depressed about anything. I mean he was happy and content. Life was good." Jasper suppressed a tear.

"So who was the mysterious young woman at the club?"

"That is the million-dollar question, or should I say billion-dollar question." Jasper made a weak attempt at levity. "Nobody can find a trace of her. I mean absolutely nothing!"

They sat silently for a couple of minutes.

"I am really sorry I didn't make it down for the funeral, Jasper. I wanted to, but I was dealing with my own parental problems, though certainly not as severe…obviously. My mother was in the hospital with something called a megacolon. Her large intestine was dilated, and she had, uh, paralysis 'down there' and couldn't, uh, relieve herself." Realizing how ridiculous it was to tell Jasper all that at a time like this, she awkwardly cleared her throat and finished up with, "Anyway, it was very serious, and she was in the hospital all week."

Jasper had been looking out the window at the countryside as they cruised along their route. "I'm sorry to hear about your mother, Mary. I'm assuming she has recovered?"

Mary nodded affirmatively as she embarrassedly finished off the now-cold twenty-ounce rest-stop coffee.

"I would say you didn't miss much, but like most events in my father's life, even his funeral was a spectacle. The news media was everywhere. And I mean they were really intrusive, asking questions about his will, his fortune, his personal life. They even went as far as speculating that my stepmother Emma might have been responsible for Dad's death and began questioning whether Emma and I would fight over the inheritance."

"And then after the terrible tragedy of Emma's suicide, all the media outlets suggested I had orchestrated it somehow. Can you believe that?"

Mary responded by furrowing her brow and shaking her head in disgust. "I saw and read all of that. Talk about fake news."

"It was nice that so many people showed up. I know some just wanted to say they were there or to be a part of the 'event,' but so many friends from the past came with honest and heartfelt words of condolence. My dad was respected. I'm sure glad Sterling was there."

Mary shot a quick glance at Jasper, feeling even guiltier about her absence. "I imagine it was nice having him around. I'm glad you guys have stayed in contact."

"He came down with Cheryl to join in on all the charity event festivities, but as it played out, he was my rock navigating the circus that ensued those next couple of days. Good ole Silver."

Mary let out a reflective sigh just as Jasper quickly turned toward her and continued, "Sterling was there. Did you know he was the one who actually saw my stepmother jump off that balcony?"

"Oh my god! What?" Mary screamed as she reactively slammed on the brakes.

"Yep. It was crazy!" exclaimed Jasper as he picked up the coffee cup that flew to his feet. He straightened up and adjusted his seat belt as Mary reset the cruise control, and the horn honking from the startled drivers around them silenced.

"Oh god! How did Sterling handle that?" Mary asked.

"Not well at all, Mary. He was a total mess. I've never seen him like that. You would have thought he saw his own mother jump."

"Speaking of Cheryl, how are the two of you getting along?" Mary asked.

"Okay, I guess. I mean, obviously, I am aware that she is not thrilled with this marriage." Jasper scoffed. "*Merwood* is a dirty word as far as she is concerned, and now, it is her daughter's last name."

"Why was Cheryl so upset with your father?" Mary tried to recall the details.

"I guess my dad tried to purchase Unbreakable Bonds and the land that surrounds it. He had plans to take it to another level, hotels, restaurants, a casino, and lakefront villas. He knew Cheryl was struggling, and he came in with a lowball offer. She was furious," Jasper recalled. "Oh, to be a fly-on-the-wall when Trish told Cheryl that we were dating."

"So do you really think Cheryl is trying to help Tricia reconcile things with you? Maybe she is jumping at this opportunity to break you up."

"I don't know. I guess I was taking her at her word," Jasper responded weakly.

"I wouldn't be surprised if Tricia never even left the farm," Mary said. She noted on the GPS that they would be arriving in less than ten minutes.

"Well, that would be nice. I have a heartfelt apology to give her." Jasper became hopeful.

Mary was less so. She was skeptical of Cheryl's intentions and planned to make Cheryl acutely aware of that skepticism.

CHAPTER 10

September 2018

Jasper and Tricia had tied the knot earlier that summer in an elegant, gorgeous ceremony in stunning Punta Cana. It had been fifteen years since Jasper's mother Paige had passed away. His father Edward and stepmother Emma were again hosting a charity gala at the expansive Merwood estate in Atlanta, Georgia.

Edward considered Emma Santo's arrival in his life just two years prior a godsend. He was on a business/pleasure yacht cruise off the Miami Beach coast when Emma, fifteen years his junior, caught his eye. Emma, the daughter of fellow real estate tycoon Ralph Santo and his wife Ronita, was by all accounts striking. She had golden-brown skin that was the envy of all her friends. Her hair bounced and flowed around her perfectly symmetrical face in the most alluring of ways. Her eyes sparkled and, despite her beauty, radiated a sweet, shy, and innocent appearance. Emma emitted joy. She was carefree and friendly and playful. Edward was intoxicated by her smile and disposition. The two hit it off over drinks in the moonlight, talking well into the morning. Edward made plans for Emma to fly to Atlanta later that week, and they never looked back.

With Emma aboard, Edward's approach to life morphed quickly. His priorities changed. He relaxed. He slowed down. He took in the smaller pleasures life had to offer as only a billionaire could—by giving money away. With Emma's prodding, he reconnected with Jasper.

Edward and Emma had made several trips to Manhattan to visit Jasper and Tricia, and likewise, the kids visited the estate in Atlanta. Tricia took advantage of this relationship to write a lengthy biographical feature that her employer, the *New York Times*, ran on the front page over the course of three straight days. The foursome got along swimmingly. They never ran out of subjects to talk about. They would hit the town and party through the evening in luxury's lap but would just as easily stay in with some wine, some games, and a nice fire. Last fall, they took a trip to the South African seaside town of Hermanus for some whale watching and then spent Christmas taking in the beauty of Salzburg, Austria.

Tricia had started referring to Emma as her "sister," a loving tongue-in-cheek reference to her age but also a compliment to the ease and comfort in which the two female Merwoods interacted.

Edward was very proud of Jasper's performance and the value he added to Merwood Real Estate and Investment Corporation. He adored Tricia and was happy for Jasper's future. He looked forward to being a grandfather, in part to make up for the absentee father he had been to Jasper, but mostly because of his renewed joy in the relationship with his only son.

On Saturday, September 1, Jasper and Tricia had once again made their way to the Merwood Estate. This time, they were in town to help get everything ready for the grand event happening one week later. Invitations had gone out to many of the rich and famous. There would be no shortage of political dignitaries, Hollywood stars, athletes, and CEOs. Local musician Zac Brown and his very successful band would be providing the entertainment. The always-immaculate grounds would be transformed into an exotic paradise with upward of half a million LED lights, ice sculptures, and separately planned lantern and butterfly releases. Fifty linen-covered tables with the finest dinnerware would surround a full circle stage and dance floor in the backyard. Guests would drink a variety of UBB wines from crystal goblets. This was the third charity function the Merwoods had hosted in the past two years, and with each event, the festivities got more and more extravagant.

Outside of a long-planned business golf/dinner outing to discuss a new luxury Merwood Tower that would add to the already-impressive skyline in Doha, Qatar, Edward's business calendar was remarkably empty. It was a wonderful feeling to be this free. He would have canceled this meeting, but the Qatar Tower was going to be the jewel of the Merwood franchise's international endeavors, and he wanted to be sure it kicked off as planned.

Edward and Emma were looking forward to some quiet time with Jasper and Tricia but also were excited for Cheryl, Sterling, and Emma's parents to arrive. There was plenty of room for everyone to stay in the six-bedroom 1880s-era mansion. The group hoped to get out and enjoy a few of the many experiences the bustling city of Atlanta provided. They knew the back end of the week would be a good bit busier as more of the party attendees made their way to A-town.

Cheryl and Sterling arrived early in the afternoon of Monday, September 3. They were picked up by a stretch limousine from the airport and enjoyed the city sights during the twenty-minute drive to the Merwood Estate, a Queen Anne-style two-story home on the list of the National Register of Historic Places by the US National Park Services on the outskirts of town. The rare-for-the-area spacious two-acre plot of land with a beautifully manicured lawn was a sight to behold. While Cheryl and Sterling were naturally aware of Edward's wealth, they were still noticeably awestruck by all they were taking in.

The driver had dropped them off at the front door where the circle driveway outlined an island of black-eyed Susan and Queen Anne's lace with a majestic water fountain in the center. Horace, the Merwoods' current butler, unloaded the car and showed them to their respective opulent bedrooms, each featuring a private bath and balcony that overlooked the grounds.

Tricia was the first to greet them, meeting them in the great room at the rear of the first floor. Four sets of French doors opened the room to a massive stone patio that separated the house from the kidney-shaped in-ground pool. Tricia ran to Sterling, and they embraced long and hard, having not seen each other since the wedding in June. Cheryl and Trisha likewise shared a loving embrace as Jasper arrived to welcome his guests. After a polite greeting with Cheryl, he and Sterling hugged affectionately. Sterling conveyed to Jasper just how astounded he was by the grandness that surrounded him. He couldn't believe Jasper had grown up in this environment. Jasper said he would trade it all to have had a normal childhood with lunch boxes, soccer games, and friends.

That evening, Edward and Emma treated all of them to quite a night on the town. They enjoyed a wonderful meal at Bowes restaurant and then took in an off-Broadway show at the TYE Center, a new theater Emma was supporting. Everyone agreed the show lived up to the hype. While sipping drinks on the rooftop bar of the Merwood Plaza in the heart of the city, the party enjoyed reminiscing about the crazy high jinks Jasper, Tricia, and Sterling got into in their time at Penn. It was a shame the night had to end, but eventually, they all climbed, staggered, or fell into the waiting limo that returned them home.

Tuesday was slower as everyone recovered. Tricia and Emma stayed busy, finalizing the gala's details. The chef was given the evening off as the men grilled steaks, potatoes, and corn. Over the satisfying dinner, the group discussed their plans for the next day. It seemed everyone had their own agenda, and transportation soon became the topic. Edward laughed and made it clear that this would not be an issue. After dessert, they all headed over to the eight-stall garage to the left of the circle driveway.

"Wow, Edward, you have quite a collection here" said Cheryl, a little put off by the opulence. "Do you and Emma drive them all?"

"Thank you. Emma likes to drive the Bentley the most, but other than those last three, when not being chauffeured, we enjoy them all." He made his way to bay number 6 and removed the cover.

"Here's my pride and joy," he bragged as he ran his fingers along the curves of the hood of the white-and-blue 1965 Shelby Mustang GT350. "This is one of only one hundred produced that first year."

Sterling whistled. "Wow. Beautiful."

"Needless to say, no one will be taking that baby out tomorrow. I've never even been allowed to sit in it." Jasper shot a sarcastic glance at his father. He then smiled, successfully concealing his resentment with jest.

"I don't need to be flashy, Edward. I'll just take the Lincoln," interjected Cheryl, ignoring Edward's motion to move toward the covered vehicles in bays number 7 and number 8.

"Oooo, I want this Jaguar," said Sterling, practically skipping over to the black convertible.

"Good choice, Silver," said Jasper. "I could tell you a lot of stories I have had with that fella." Turning to Trish, he asked, "Since Emma has the Bentley, would you prefer the trusty Mercedes SUV or the less-pretentious coupé?"

Trish stood there for a moment of exaggerated dramatic pause, then answered, "My dear, let's take the SUV for our daytime errands and the coupé for our evening out. Since I'm changing clothes, I might as well also change the accessories."

The Merwoods and their guests were in a jovial mood as they made their way back to the house to relax for the evening.

*****

On Wednesday, September 5, Edward was up early. His partners from Qatar had arrived very late the prior night, and a company driver dropped them at the luxurious Ritz-Carlton downtown. That morning, they were picked up and driven to meet Edward for breakfast at the country club before teeing off on the beautifully maintained world-class course. Dinner would follow at the elite Georgian Club, and the Qataris would be back on a flight across the Atlantic by late evening.

Emma left for the airport that morning. Her parents, Ralph and Ronita, were arriving from Miami, and she had a full day of activities planned with them.

Jasper, Tricia, Cheryl, and Sterling were quite happy to laze much of the morning and early afternoon. After sleeping in, they ate breakfast poolside. They read books, magazines, and newspapers; they played on their phones. The temperature was a warm eighty-five degrees, and occasionally, they would jump in and cool off. This was the most fun Jasper had had in his childhood home. It was a good day.

Jasper and Tricia had planned to patronize a recently opened seafood restaurant that evening and invited Cheryl and Sterling along, but each already had plans and declined.

Cheryl was very excited about an evening of pampering. She was getting her hair and nails done and decided to add in a deep tissue massage for good measure. Even though she had packed her best clothes for the festivities, she realized her wardrobe did not match the Merwood style, so she announced she would need to do some shopping.

Sterling and a friend who lived in nearby Milledgeville, Georgia, were going to meet up and take in the Braves vs the Red Sox game that evening. Sterling was dressed in all his blue-and-red glory including his retro hat, Carl Yastrzemski jersey, and matching pair of red socks.

After picking up a few things from the catering company for Emma, Jasper and Tricia enjoyed their private date night feasting on lobster tail and tuna steaks. They followed this up with a walk through Centennial Park and a romantic ride on the Skyview Atlanta, a twenty-story, two-hundred-foot-high Ferris wheel that allowed a 360-degree scenic view of the city.

"What a beautiful evening, Jasper. Thank you," said Tricia as she snuggled in close. There was a pleasant breeze that high over the city. She pulled out her phone and took a picture of the two of them towering over the city lights.

"I love you, Tricia. This has been an amazing year for us so far. I am so lucky to have you in my life. I can't wait to see what life has in store for us." He pulled Trish in even closer and kissed her forehead. *Life is good.*

*****

Edward was walking his Qatari business associates out to the waiting car when the bartender caught his attention. "Mr. Merwood, can I see you for a moment?"

"Let me say goodbye to my friends, and I will be right back."

He gave each of his visitors a hearty handshake as they entered the limousine that would take them to the airport. "Have a safe trip, gentlemen. I'm looking forward to this arrangement."

Edward stopped to tell his own driver that he would be back in a few minutes, and he headed back into the club. "Hi, Ben, what can I do for you?"

"A woman was waiting here for you. She bought you this drink," he replied, pointing to the mint julep on the bar.

"Really? Did she tell you her name?" asked Edward as he took a seat in front of the drink.

"Jan."

"Jan? Hmmm…I don't know anyone named Jan. What did she look like?"

With a smile, the bartender described the woman as young and beautiful. She had long black curly hair and wore glasses. She was alone and engaged in pleasant conversation but did not reveal how she knew Edward Merwood.

"Doesn't ring a bell. Must be someone who came in for the fundraiser tomorrow." Edward picked up the drink, gave a ceremonious toast into the air, "Here's to giving money away," and he downed the beverage. "See you soon, Ben." He tapped the bar top in satisfaction of a great evening as he swiveled the chair around and headed out the door.

"Let's head home," he told his waiting driver.

*****

Jasper and Tricia were out relatively late and were surprised to return home to an empty house. She quipped, "And we thought we knew how to party." Jasper lit the fireplace in the great room, and they relaxed together on the oversize couch awaiting the return of the rest of the family.

Shortly thereafter, there was a knock on the door. Horace had long since retired to his quarters, so Tricia answered. Jasper's heart fell as Trish ushered two uniformed police officers into the foyer. The officers proceeded to explain that Edward had been rushed to the hospital by his limo driver after suddenly becoming unresponsive on the ride home from dinner. He was gone. Jasper nearly collapsed on the spot. Trish and one of the officers helped him to a chair in the living room, and Trish went for some water and a cold washcloth.

In a whirlwind, Jasper and Tricia were given a police escort to Grady Memorial Hospital and sent out notification of the horrific news to the rest of the group while en route.

Jasper broke down uncontrollably at the sight of his father on the nondescript hospital gurney with the sheet drawn up to his neck. Things were going so perfectly. Jasper finally had a loving, caring, interested, participating, proud father in his life. Now, he was gone.

Cheryl was the next to arrive. She looked out of place in a beautiful new full-length black dress with rhinestones and her every-day sandals. She explained that she was in the dressing room at Nordstrom's when she got Trish's text. She ran out, threw cash on the counter, and rushed to the hospital. Cheryl offered her deepest con-dolences to Jasper and repeatedly expressed what a shame this was.

Emma and her parents arrived soon after. Emma was clearly in shock, but the tears still flowed freely. Jasper hugged his stepmother tightly and tried unsuccessfully to console her. It was going to be a long recovery for the newly constructed Merwood family.

Sterling was the last of the group to show up at the hospital. He found Jasper in a waiting room area staring blankly into a vending machine. When Jasper spotted him, he said, "I don't know what to do." Sterling gave his buddy a warm hug and said, "You're going to make your dad proud." Then, he clicked the button next to the bar-beque potato chips and watched the bag drop to the tray. Sterling's father, Roger Shapiro, had passed away just a couple of years earlier; he knew from experience how to support his best friend now.

*****

The charity event was off, but most of the guests would stay in town for the funeral of one of the most prominent business tycoons in the world.

The next couple of days were a blur: obituary writing, funeral preparations, calling hours, and endless phone calls offering thoughts, prayers, and condolences. Not to mention the media covering what was supposed to be a charitable gala now-turned funeral.

An autopsy of Edward had turned up lethal levels of barbiturates. An investigation into the events of the evening had begun in earnest. The family was questioned. The Qataris were questioned. The staff members at the club were questioned. The bartender told investigators that a young woman with long black hair had convinced Edward to meet her for a moment at the bar and purchased drinks. When Edward arrived at the bar, the girl had left. Was Edward's drink tainted? Identification of this woman was the key to the investigation.

While thousands showed up to the funeral itself, only a select few of no more than twenty guests were invited back to the Merwood estate for a private reception.

The guests were mingling in the great room before the meal, picking at hors d'oeuvres, drinking cocktails, and having hushed conversations. Emma had been absent since returning from the cemetery. She had not slept in days. Her private physician prescribed her Valium, and she told Horace she needed some time to herself. The minister was preparing to leave and wanted to offer Emma final condolences. Ronita and Cheryl left in search of Emma.

Jasper walked up to Sterling and asked if they could discuss some business. He informed Sterling that he had been contacted by a number of his father's investors the prior afternoon. He needed some sound advice from someone he trusted. He asked him to meet in the private second-floor study.

Sterling climbed the stairs while Jasper stopped to pour two vodka tonics.

*****

Moments later, Sterling and Jasper were racing outside with many confused and frightened guests in tow. Emma had landed face-first in the garden beneath a second-story balcony, and her lifeless body was horrifying in contrast to the beautiful collection of award-winning varieties of roses. There was no attempt to resuscitate as it was visible from the mess caused when her head hit one of the many rocks in the garden that she did not survive the fall. Her father, Ralph, broke down in mournful sobs, and her mother Ronita fainted at the sight.

Later, when Jasper, Tricia, Cheryl, and Sterling were alone, Sterling, still in shock, tried to recount the final seconds of Emma's life that he had been unwittingly and unfortunate enough to have witnessed. Everyone was aware and sympathetic of Emma's grief since Edward's unexpected death, but nobody suspected that the carefree, generous soul was capable of this.

A week that had started out as a celebration of giving had concluded in tragic loss.

CHAPTER 11

December 22, 2018, 2:00 PM

Your destination is on the left. The GPS indicated the turn that would lead Jasper and Mary up to UBB's main house. "Well, here we are," Jasper said. "Mary, I truly hope this is all a false alarm, and we find Tricia sitting on the couch watching an episode of *American Pickers* with her mother."

Even though Mary was a college friend of Tricia's, she had never been to the farm. At the gate, Mary pushed the buzzer button connected to a brick wall with a stone placard that announced, "*Unbreakable Bonds: established 1960.*" A man's voice was heard through the speaker, "May I help you?"

Mary replied, "Jasper Merwood and Mary Sintag to see Cheryl Maxwell. She is expecting us."

A few seconds later, the majestic wrought-iron fence opened from the middle, splitting the large calligraphy *M* to each side. As she slowly steered along the gravel driveway, Mary took in a deep breath.

The farm grounds were beautiful, even in the winter. White fences created a mosaic on the left, separating the different riding arenas for the stables. On the right, beyond an orderly row of barren trees that stood about twenty feet high was a grove of pine trees showing off their evergreen needles against the snowy landscape. The sign up ahead pointed the driver to the direction of the stables, the winery, the farm shed, or the Maxwell house. Mary turned slightly left, and the main house came into view. It was not an elaborate mansion one would expect to see for such a successful estate, but it was breathtaking nonetheless. The one-and-a-half-story stone home had a full-length front porch with oversized white columns supporting the roof. Christmas wreaths decorated the windows, each adorned with a burgundy-and-gold bow.

The temperature had dropped dramatically during the six-hour journey to wine country, so Jasper and Mary reached in the back seat for their coats before exiting the car. Mary followed Jasper along the curved cobblestone sidewalk and couldn't help but think what a beautiful place for a white Christmas. She pictured a horse-drawn sleigh carrying riders along the country estate while jingle bells sounded from the harnesses.

Jasper, on the other hand, had allowed himself to become hopeful the last few minutes of the drive. He was picturing his beautiful wife greeting him at the door. Today was her birthday, and Jasper put his hand in his pocket to feel the wrapped jewelry box that contained a ruby heart-shaped pendant on a silver chain that he had purchased for her. But as they approached, Jasper noted the absence of Trish's car and was deflated.

Mary's daydream was abruptly stalled when she heard Jasper clear his throat and let out a deep breath as they made their way up the steps to the front door. Before he could knock, the door opened.

"Jasper, I don't know why you came all the way out here. I told you Tricia isn't here," was the greeting Cheryl gave Jasper and Mary. Cheryl was not pleased with this impromptu visit since just arriving home in the wee hours of the morning from a business trip. She had only listened to Jasper's voice mail fifteen minutes prior. Barely having enough time for a quick shower, Cheryl stood at the entryway in a white terry robe and her hair wrapped in a towel.

As Mary extended a hand in greeting, Jasper said, "Cheryl, you remember Mary Sintag, Tricia's friend from college. She's a private investigator now."

"I remember you, Mary. What possibly brings you to UBB today?" replied Cheryl as she cinched the collar of her robe a little tighter. "Do you get called into these kinds of domestic squabble cases often?"

"Hello again, Cheryl. Jasper has good reason to feel this is much more serious than that. Trish hasn't made it home, and we can't reach her by phone. Can you tell us when the last time was you saw your daughter?" Mary wasn't one to waste time on pleasantries; the private investigator instincts in her had immediately taken over.

Turning her attention to Jasper, Cheryl responded, "This is crazy. Maybe if you spent a little less time at the office or in the bars, you wouldn't be in this predicament."

"Ma'am, the last time you saw Tricia?" Mary persisted.

With a softer tone, Cheryl took their coats and stated, "Let's have some coffee."

Cheryl led her visitors down the wide hallway from the foyer to the kitchen. Out of the corner of her eye, Mary spotted a majestic Christmas tree rising to the vaulted ceiling of the living room. Decorated in all white lights with burgundy-and-gold bulbs, the tree gave off an ambiance of elegance and peace.

"Like I told Jasper, the last time I saw Tricia would have been Thursday around 11:00 AM." Cheryl reached into one of the tall pine cabinets and removed three coffee mugs. She poured the hot coffee and handed one to each of her guests. She motioned for them to sit at the table where sugar and creamer were arranged on a lazy Susan in the center.

"Are you not worried about your daughter at all?" asked Mary as she added two cubes of sugar to her brew.

Matter-of-factly, Cheryl answered, "I am not. When Trish gets mad at me, she leaves, and I never know when I'll hear from her again. Look, Trish is very upset, and she has cause to be. I understand what you have been through the last few months is unspeakable, and

I can only imagine what you are feeling. But Tricia has been there for you throughout. You need to treat her better. She deserves that."

Jasper nodded solemnly, but Mary persisted. "Cheryl, did Tricia tell you what her plans were before she left?"

"I had listened to Tricia go on and on about her frustration with Jasper, but she wasn't willing to do anything about it except sit here and mope. She got angry with me when I stopped coddling her and suggested either she accepts the marriage for what it is"—Cheryl gave a disapproving sideways glance at Jasper—"or do something about it. She got huffy and said she was leaving. I assumed that meant she was going back to Jasper to address their problems one way or another."

"So she never actually said she was going back to Jasper?" Mary questioned.

Cheryl thought for a second. "Well, she did in a roundabout way. She said she would take her time and get there eventually."

"But, Cheryl, today's her birthday," Jasper interjected. "Certainly, she would have made contact with one of us."

Cheryl didn't have time to respond as just then, the phone rang. "I bet that's her now."

Cheryl picked up. "Oh, good afternoon, Sterling... Yes, I got back very early this morning... That is Jasper's car. He is here with Mary Sintag. They are looking for Trish. I told them she left here Thursday. Are you sure that's a good idea? Okay...of course. I will send him down."

Cheryl hung up and said, "Jasper, that was Sterling. He is very excited to see you and would like you to come down to the stables."

Mary said, "Jasper, you go ahead down and see Sterling. I am also very excited to see the silver bullet, but for now, I would like to stay here and ask Cheryl a few more questions to see if we can figure out where Tricia is hiding."

*****

Jasper started down to the stables, and as he got close, Sterling came out, brush in one hand, shovel in the other, sweat pouring off in buckets.

"Better hope that sweat doesn't freeze. You will be one big popsicle," Jasper joked as the two friends embraced warmly.

"Sure beats sweating in July. So I understand you can't find Trish."

"No, sir. I was really hoping I would find her here."

"I'll tell you, Jams, she was really frustrated about everything. She feels awful about all you are going through. She feels hopeless and useless. It sure has been a rocky start to this marriage," Sterling opined.

"You're telling me. You know, Silver, it seems you and I only see each other in times of tragedy. I really appreciate you being here for me. Tell you what, I'm going to find Trish, fix this mess, and then you and I will get together, put a few back, and pretend we are at the frat house back at Penn."

As if on cue, Sterling went over to a small refrigerator in the stable office and grabbed a couple of Bud Lights and tossed one to Jasper. The two men then walked over to a nearby workbench and took a seat. Popping the tops of the beers, Sterling toasted, "To finding Trish." He took a big hearty swig.

"To be honest, Jasper, it has been nice having Tricia around here for a couple of days, even under these circumstances. I missed you guys at Thanksgiving."

"Well, Trish certainly planned on us coming up here, but I begged for a more low-key holiday at home. We needed the quality time. Man, Silver, did I screw that up. I have really been a mess since...," Jasper's voice cracked a bit, and he did not finish the thought.

"I am still so sorry about all that you have been through, buddy," Sterling attempted comfort. "I think about it all the time."

"Thanks, Silver, but it is time for me to move on. I can't keep feeling sorry for myself. It doesn't help anyone, and Trish was so patient and understanding. Day after day, she put up with my detachment, my sulking, and my short temper. This was when I was around, which really wasn't much.

"She took care of everything around the house, and she took care of me, especially since I wasn't taking care of myself. She made sure I ate. She got me into bed when I would come home drunk and pass out on the living room floor.

"She did everything, Silver. She begged me to come back to her. She begged to go to dinner, to go to a movie, to just sit down together and watch a television show, and I couldn't. No, I should say, I wouldn't…," and again, Jasper's voice trailed off.

Sterling broke in, "Jams, I know Trish loves you."

As if not even hearing Sterling, Jasper reminisced, "You remember the night Trish and I met?"

"Of course, I do." Sterling laughed. "I was the sexiest, tallest jockey that ever was."

"Certainly, the tallest!" responded Jasper with a brief smile. "Trish and I connected so immediately that night. It was like nothing I've ever felt before. We had this innate bond. We were soul mates. We were always on the same page. We would have the same thoughts at the same time or even feel each other's pain or happiness even when we were not together. We were meant to be. It has been like that ever since…well…until the last four months or so."

"I saw it firsthand, man. I never saw any two people so destined to be together. But let's face it, you have changed."

Jasper started to cry. "Where did she go, Sterling? I need to find her."

Sterling looked perplexed and pained at seeing his friend like this. He hugged Jasper and said, "We will. We will find her."

After a moment, Jasper regained his composure and said, "Silver, let's figure this out. When did you see Tricia last? When did she leave? She was coming home, right?"

"I'm pretty sure she was…or at least, I assumed she was. At one point, I remember her saying she couldn't wait to have a slice of real pizza again."

"And she definitely left on Thursday?"

"I'm sure of it."

Jasper questioned, "So then, where is she? Did she say she was going to drop down to any of the old college haunts in Philly?"

"Nope. No mention of anything like that," answered Sterling.

Jasper looked puzzled. "She really doesn't have any friends between here and Manhattan except for our mutual friends in the city...all of whom I have checked with. Mary is just as concerned. She's here with me."

"I heard. I can't wait to say hello!" Sterling exclaimed.

"Is it possible she had car trouble or ran out of gas? Shoot... maybe she stopped to help somebody on the road, and they took her phone, and...and they..." Back to tears, Jasper's imagination was running wild with possibilities that could be keeping Tricia from him.

Sterling patted his friend on the shoulder. "Jasper, I checked the car out. It was in great condition. I filled it with gas, checked the tires, and even got it a tune-up. Trish mentioned she was overdue for an oil change and was worried about a rattling she was hearing. So while she was packing, I took the car up to Eddie Mac's and had Jimmy take a quick look. The rattling was just a stone stuck in the wheel well. She was safe, man. Don't worry about that."

Jasper continued, "Maybe an accident?"

"We would have heard about an accident, Jasper."

"I don't know, Silver. I am going crazy."

Sterling, looking a little bewildered, finally said, "I can't believe this is happening."

Jasper smacked his hands on his knees as he stood up. "It's getting cold out here. Let's head to the house and see if Cheryl and Mary are getting anywhere."

*****

Jasper and Sterling made their way into the house and found the women still seated at the kitchen table.

"Well? Anything?" Jasper said without greeting.

"Nothing really," answered Mary as she gave Sterling a big hug on her way to put her coffee mug in the sink.

"We need to file a missing-person report and get some help in this search."

Cheryl put a gentle hand on Jasper's shoulder. "I am very worried about Tricia myself. But as I was just telling Mary a few moments ago, Trish does have a history of running off when she gets angry with me. Give me a little time to make some calls around town and see if I can learn anything before we involve the authorities."

Jasper reluctantly agreed. "Mary and I will go check into the Lake View Motel. It's probably the only place open during the off-season. You have one hour, and then, I am going to the police station."

"Jasper, if you would have given me more notice, you could have stayed here. Sorry, but I'm just not prepared to host the two of you. Nonetheless, there is no need to stay at such a seedy place. I will give my friends Harry and Susan Broadmoar a call. They own the Oak Barrel Bed and Breakfast in Fredonia, and they can put you and Mary up for the night."

"Thanks, Cheryl. Tell them we're on our way." Jasper gave Sterling a nod goodbye and headed toward the door.

Mary blurted as she hustled to catch up to Jasper, "Maybe we can stop for a quick lunch? I could really go for a steak sandwich."

CHAPTER 12

December 22, 2018, 3:30 PM

The B&B gets quiet this time of year, and Harry and Susan Broadmoar were delighted to accommodate Cheryl Maxwell's request to host her son-in-law and Tricia's college friend. To save on heating costs in the century-old two-story frame house overlooking Lake Erie, they closed the upstairs bedrooms for the winter but always kept the guest suite on the first floor ready for unexpected visitors.

*****

Cheryl answered on the third ring. "Hi, Jasper. Are you situated over there at the Oak Barrel?"

Jasper ignored the question and the formalities. "Cheryl, any luck? What have you learned?"

Taken aback by his bluntness, she stated matter-of-factly, "I put feelers out all over town. I spoke to some friends as well as the local business owners who know Tricia. Everyone is aware that I have gone and upset her again. They know we are worried about her, and that you are in town looking for her.

"Jasper, I understand you are very concerned," Cheryl continued in a calmer, reassuring voice. "But Trish is okay. Once she finds out you are here, she will reach out. By this time tomorrow, you two will be together. I am sure of it. I mean, I'm her mother. Certainly, I would sense if something was wrong."

"Thanks, Cheryl. I hope you are right," was all Jasper said before clicking off and turning to Mary. "Let's go. It is time to fill out a missing-person report."

"Sounds good," Mary responded, gathering up her deli wrappers, tossing them in the garbage, and heading for the door.

*****

The Westfield Police Department was located on Elm Street, about a twenty-minute drive from the B&B. Jasper and Mary entered the two-story red-brick front entrance guarded by four large white pillars and headed to the receptionist's desk. They were met warmly by a young lady with oversize glasses and long dangly earrings. "How may I help you?" she asked, followed by a loud snap of her chewing gum.

After indicating they needed to file a missing-person report, Bubbles, as Jasper and Mary would later refer to her, led them to the desk of Officer Curtis Jancy. Officer Jancy was finishing up a report and acknowledged Jasper and Mary with a raised finger, indicating to hold on a moment.

As Jasper and Mary settled into their chairs, they took in the surroundings. The precinct floor was a maze of desks identical to the one they were at now, desks with one large chair and one or two smaller chairs for visitors. The far wall housed two large offices, one marked "Chief of Police" and the other marked "Sergeant." On the wall opposite the windows was a conference room with a large table in the center and a podium in front adjacent to a whiteboard. Beyond the conference room was a small kitchen housing two round tables and several vending machines. What the office lacked at this moment, it appeared, were police officers as most of the cluttered desks were empty.

Officer Jancy finished his report and then spun his chair to face Jasper and Mary. "Hi, can I help the two of you? I understand that we have a missing person."

Jasper nodded affirmatively and responded, "That's right. My wife has not been seen for several days now, and her phone is going straight to voice mail."

As Officer Jancy fed a preprinted form into the antiquated typewriter, he asked, "What is your wife's full name, and where was she last seen?"

"Patricia Maxwell Merwood and she was last seen leaving the Unbreakable Bonds main house on Thursday morning."

Officer Jancy looked up, surprised. "Trisha Maxwell?"

Jasper nodded.

"I know Trish very well. Our family was good friends with the Maxwells. My brother Wesley was closer to Tricia than I was. I believe Wes and Trish actually had a thing for each other back in junior high." Jasper's look told Officer Jancy he was not amused with the reminiscing. "Oh, man, I'm sorry to hear this. Cheryl must be pretty upset."

Jasper shook his head in disagreement. "She is not as worried as I am. She thinks Trish is upset with her and just staying away for a bit. She said it has happened before."

Officer Jancy remembered, "Come to think of it, I do think there was a time back in high school when she spent a couple of nights at our place after a fight with her mom."

"Maybe that's all this is, but I don't think so. Mary and I agree that this is something more. We think Trish may be in danger, and we need your help."

Officer Jancy shook Mary's hand. "Hello, Mary. Are you family?"

"No, Sir. I'm an old college friend of Tricia's...and a private investigator from Manhattan."

"Mary Sintag?"

"That's me."

"Well, I'll be darn! I've read all about the work you did to help track down the Central Park killer! That was pretty impressive how you picked up on the shoelaces."

"Thank you. I was just really glad that I was able to help. The CPK was definitely the scariest bad guy I have come in contact with in my police work to date."

"You worked in the public sector as well?"

"Foot patrol on Long Island for a bit. I enjoy this more."

"Well, it's an honor to meet you. Now, let's get this report started and find Trish." Turning back to Jasper, he continued, "You said she was leaving UBB?" Jasper nodded in affirmation. "Do you know what she was driving?"

"It was a red Ford Mustang convertible, nothing really special about it except for a silver scrape on the driver's side."

Officer Jancy typed away as Jasper relayed the details as he knew them. He spent the next twenty minutes answering the rest of the standard questions. The only piece of information Jasper could not produce was Tricia's license plate number. He promised to get that information tomorrow, but Officer Jancy said he could pull it up online. In the meantime, he said he would issue an alert across New York, the bordering states, and Canada to get police officers on the lookout for a slender woman with short dark-brown hair in her twenties driving a red Ford Mustang.

As Jasper and Mary left the station, they agreed it had already been a long and exhausting day. They decided to get some rest at the B&B.

*****

Two hours later, Jasper and Mary were seated at Manning's Fireside Manor in Dunkirk, sharing pan-seared salmon and garlic clam pasta on the recommendation of the Broadmoars. They spent several hours rehashing what they already knew. Mary checked online and confirmed that as of Thursday morning, the New York State Highway Patrol's website was not listing any accidents along the route they suspected Tricia would have taken driving home. *Where was Tricia?*

Approaching midnight, Jasper got a call. The caller identified himself as Officer Winston from the Westfield Police Department.

He had received Officer Jancy's APB on Tricia and her car…and he had information about the car. As it turns out, Trish's vehicle had been found this afternoon in the train station's parking lot. It was being towed to the Westfield municipal impound lot.

Mary watched as Jasper's face contorted and displayed confusion. He was clearly surprised at the news he was receiving.

After thanking the officer and hanging up the phone, Jasper relayed the information to Mary.

"Well, that doesn't make any sense, Jasper," Mary said. "Tricia and Sterling were getting that car ready for the cross-state journey. How did it end up at the local train station?"

Jasper didn't respond to Mary as the phone was already at his ear. "Hi, Cheryl, it's Jasper. We just got a call from the police. They found Trish's car at the train station. Please call me as soon as you can."

"Jasper, I don't think we are getting the full story." Mary continued, "Tomorrow, I think we need to go back to the farm and pay Sterling another visit."

CHAPTER 13

December 23, 2018, 1:00 AM

Jasper and Mary made plans to get up early in the morning. They would head back to UBB at 7:00 AM sharp. Now, Jasper was sure that something was wrong, and that Tricia was in danger—or worse. Up until Officer Winston's call, while Jasper was worried about Trish, in the back of his mind, he was confident that there was a logical explanation, and that everything would be okay. Cheryl was right, and Jasper was overreacting. But now, everything was different. Trish had told Cheryl and Sterling that she was going for a long drive, yet her car was found just a few miles away. *Where had she gone? What had happened to her? Had she been kidnapped? Was she alive?*

*****

Ring. Voice mail. Tricia's phone was still shut off. This time though, Jasper left a voice mail.

"Trish, it's me again. Please call me back. I miss you so much. I am so sorry for being a jerk and causing you pain these past few months. I need you. I love you. Happy birthday, my dear sweet wife."

*****

As he lay in bed, Jasper pictured Tricia on her way home to Manhattan when she spots another driver stopped along Route 5, seemingly in distress, flagging her down for help. When Trish pulls over, a man jumps from the trees, gets in her car, and holds her at gunpoint. He orders her to drive them to the train station.

Jasper shook his head and silently told himself to stop that. He would never get to sleep thinking like this. He tried to put positive imagery in his mind. He pictured Trish returning home and a long embrace. He pictured the two of them cuddled up warmly under a blanket in front of the fireplace opening Christmas presents. Finally, exhaustion from what had been an extremely long day took its toll, and Jasper fell asleep.

Jasper's subconscious mind took over, and he was suddenly on a wild ride through the last six years of his life, the Trish years, alternating between happy and sad memories, exciting and terrifying memories…so many memories.

*****

"Thank you, Mrs. Maxwell. You have such a beautiful home. I really appreciate you putting me up. I hope I will be seeing a lot more of you in the future," Jasper says, sneaking a look and a wink at his beautiful girlfriend, Tricia.

"You are more than welcome, Jasper. It has been my pleasure. You and Trish make such a perfect couple. Almost too perfect," Cheryl adds with a laugh.

"Silver, I will see you in a couple of weeks. You better get some training in, or you won't have a shot of keeping up with me in the pool this year."

"Ha-ha, we will see about that, Jammers. Have a safe trip back to Wharton. See you soon."

Jasper jumps in his shiny silver Camaro and waves goodbye.

*****

Trish jumps from her new shiny red Ford Mustang, the spoils of her new job with the New York Times, *and runs to Jasper's car.*

"I love it!" exclaims Jasper.

"So do I! So do I!" shouts Trish, jumping into his arms.

"Let me see what it can do." Jasper jumps in and starts the engine, and Trish playfully drops her arms to signal the start of the race.

*****

Jasper, looking like John Travolta in Grease, *is racing down Thunderbird Road when he catches sight in the distance of the Pink Ladies cheering him on. Upon winning the race in a twist, it is Stockard Channing's tough girl Rizzo who gets to Jasper first and not the expected Olivia Newton-John. Travolta and Channing embrace warmly.*

*****

Jasper and Trish break from a warm hug. It is graduation weekend at Penn.

"We did it, Jammers!"

"We sure did, baby! Now, it's off to the Big Apple." Jasper starts singing, "If we can make it there…"

"We can make it anywhere!" Trish finishes as they toss their caps into the air.

*****

Jasper watches as the stone he just tossed skips across the water. He is suddenly on the shore of Lake Erie in the beautiful, relaxing, and historic gated community of Van Buren Point. Jasper and Tricia have been fortunate to spend a week at Maple Oak on Central Avenue. The cottage is owned by great family friends of the Maxwells, the Winchester family. Peg was more than happy to open her home to the budding couple.

"Hurry up, Jasper!" Trish calls. "I don't want to be late for bingo night at the community center."

"No, ma'am, don't want to miss that." Jasper laughs. "Before..."

"B-4, what?" jokes Trish.

"Before bingo, I want to get a picture of you down by the Mark Twain cottage and in front of Pulpit Rock before that cliff has completely weathered away."

"Good thinking." Trish giggles as she runs up ahead.

*****

Trish races ahead of Jasper, taking the steps of Columbia University's Low Memorial Library two at a time toward the ten majestic pillars that guard its entrance.

"Best birthday present EVER!" she spouts between breaths. "I can't believe we are invited guests to the Pulitzer Prize Awards!"

"Professor Samuels always took a liking to me. I'm just glad he had the connections to pull the strings," Jasper says calmly, trying to hide the overwhelming feeling of joyful satisfaction.

"C'mon, Jasper. Hurry up. I don't want to miss a single thing."

*****

Trish is almost pulling Jasper along as she heads down the beautiful beach access point off Lakeside Road. The path leads to a bench, which is the perfect place to watch the majestic sunsets that often grace Van Buren Point. It also leads to a staircase that takes you down the cliff to the stone-covered beach.

"C'mon, Jammers. This is going to be the best sunset yet. Look how red the sky is!"

"Almost as red as that amazing lake glass piece you found this afternoon," noted Jasper.

As they get to the bench, they take it all in with deep breaths and mental photography. Trish in awe says, "What artistry! What beauty God has provided for us!"

"It is beautiful, Trish, but not as beautiful as you."

"Oh, Jammers, you are so corny," Trish starts as she spins around to face Jasper and finds him on bended knee.

"Tricia, I have never felt so loved as I feel with you. I have never been more happy or more at peace. We fit together like the last two pieces in a jigsaw puzzle. I love you with all my heart. I want you in my life forever. Trish, will you complete my puzzle?" And with that, Jasper produces a four-carat stone, the likes Trish has never seen before.

"Of course, I will! Jammers, you make me so happy. I cannot imagine a single day without you!"

After a long embrace, they descend the steps toward the stone-covered beach.

*****

Jasper steps out onto the stunning white sandy beach of the Caribbean Sea, straightens his sky-blue bow tie and tugs at his long white tuxedo. He spies his gorgeous bride-to-be Trish. It is another beautiful day in the Dominican Republic's lavish all-inclusive Punta Cana resort. Jasper takes his spot in front of the elaborate arch-shaped trellis covered in fragrant white lilies. A few moments later, the preacher says, "Jasper, do you take Patricia to be your lawfully wedded—"

*****

"I do!" Jasper yells when Sterling asks if anyone wants to head back to the beach to watch the sunset.

"I'm coming too," says Trish as most of the guests chose to stay at the bar.

The sun is a huge glowing red-orange ball as it makes its way to bed in the western sky. Jasper and Trish watch as the sun sinks into the sea.

"What an unbelievable wedding." Trish sighs contentedly.

"What an unbelievable life," Jasper says, matching her sigh. "And to think...this is only the beginning."

They continue to hold each other in total bliss as the light begins to dim.

*****

In the dimly lit Bobby G's bar in uptown Manhattan, Jasper slurs, "Hit me up, bubby," awkwardly lifting his glass and dropping two ice cubes to the floor.

"I think you've had enough, Jasper. I've called you a cab. Let's get you home to that beautiful wife of yours."

"Is till urly jet," Jasper says as he wobbles slightly, catching himself on the neighboring barstool.

Bobby watches as Jasper staggers a weaving path to the door.

*****

Jasper stumbles through the door and into the living room. He almost makes the couch, but comes up short, clanking his head off the coffee table as his body painfully lands on the floor. This is not new, and Tricia comes in fully aware of what she will find.

"Jasper, when is this going to stop?" she asks desperately, more to herself than Jasper. "Oh, honey, you are bleeding!"

Trish heads to the kitchen to get a washcloth and cold compress. She returns to Jasper and washes away some blood.

"Get off me, woman!" Jasper shouts and tries to push Trish away. "I don't feel well. Just let me be."

Jasper tries to stand up, but he can't muster the strength and collapses back to the floor. He is feeling dizzy and light-headed; he can't seem to find the oxygen to stay awake. Trish tries again to comfort him.

"Go away!" are the last words Jasper says, and tears streaming down Tricia's cheeks are his last sight before fading off into unconsciousness.

"Jasper, wake up! Wake up!"

CHAPTER 14

Mary's Thoughts

Mary and Jasper had said good night and entered their respective bedroom areas off the sitting room of the guest suite at the Oak Barrel Bed and Breakfast. Their hosts, Harry and Susan, had already retired for the night. It had been a long day, and Mary couldn't wait to get a shower and fall into the green-and-tan plaid fluffy-looking bed awaiting her.

*****

    Even though exhausted, Mary lay awake, staring at the pine trees, the pine garland, and the pine cones that heavily decorated her room. *Boy, for living in wine country, Susan really likes pine more than grapes.*

    Officer Winston's revelation that Tricia's car was found in Westfield was devastating in Mary's mind. She needed to gather her thoughts, and she couldn't express them to Jasper just yet. She knew tomorrow's conversation with Sterling was a vital piece in this investigation. Mary needed to hear Sterling tell his story in person…to look him in the eye. She couldn't put her finger on this yet, and that bothered her.

Sterling, what aren't you telling us?

Mary's mind shifted to her relationship with Tricia. They had been the best of friends that first year at Penn. They were inseparable. Now, despite living just a short drive apart, they were Facebook friends and not much more.

Trish, where are you? I am so sorry I wasn't here for you in your time of need. How could I have let this happen?

The question was rhetorical. Mary knew the answer: Jasper. Jasper Merwood happened.

Jasper, how are you oblivious to the fact that I love you?

The thought made her sad, and a tear squeezed from her eye. Mary had been dealing with her insatiable feelings for Jasper ever since their first meeting at that Halloween party six long years ago. He was gorgeous, and he was supposed to be hers that night. As she had so many times before, Mary began to consider what life would have been like for her and Jasper if fate hadn't stepped in with Tricia Maxwell.

Jasper was pure and genuine and sincere. He was confident and respected and smart…and oh, so very handsome!

Jasper's inner circle was small, and Mary should have felt privileged to be in it. But it actually made things worse. It felt more like a prison. Day after day, she lived with the pain of loving someone who was in love with someone else, and that someone else was also her best friend. She couldn't do it anymore. She dropped out of college. She minimized contact with Trish. She focused on her career.

Jasper, I didn't miss your wedding for a client. No, man, I couldn't bear to be there when you married Trish. Instead, I stayed home and cried. I cried until I was sick.

Mary flopped to her other side while adjusting her pillow. These thoughts were making her sick now.

What am I doing here? Why did I put myself through this torture of being with you instead of referring you to someone else for help finding Trish? I am not strong enough for this. I love you, Jasper.

Mary suddenly realized she had indeed made herself ill. She jumped from her bed and stumbled to the bathroom just in time for her semidigested dinner to get flushed down the toilet.

Getting sick while thinking of Jasper was nothing new, but this was different. She felt so weak, as if oxygen-depleted. She mustered just enough energy to make it over to the bathroom window and threw it open. After a few deep breaths of the cool winter air, she began to recover.

I need to get to Jasper...now!

CHAPTER 15

December 23, 2018, 3:00 AM

"Jasper, wake up! Wake up!" Mary was shaking Jasper. He wasn't responding.

Mary ran over to the bedroom windows, unlatched the locks, and opened them both. She took in a deep breath. She then went back to the unconscious Jasper. Pulling him sideways to the edge of the bed, she locked both arms under his and dragged him from the bed over to the waiting crisp air.

"Come on, Jasper, breathe!" Mary was holding Jasper's head out the open window. She glanced around outside. It was dark except for the glow from the kitchen light that their hosts had left on for them. The night was still; Mary didn't hear a sound.

"Breathe, Jasper!" yelled Mary again as she continued to shake him while holding her own head out the window. Finally, Jasper let out a moan and a cough.

"Jasper, Jasper, are you with me, buddy?" Mary pleaded.

"What's going on, Mary?" Jasper asked weakly.

"I'll explain everything. But first, take a few more deep breaths. We have to get to Harry and Susan NOW!"

*****

Red, white, and blue lights bounced off the white exterior of the Oak Barrel Bed and Breakfast. Fire trucks, ambulances, and police cars responded to the 911 call Mary had made. The snow was coming down and accumulating quickly. Bundled in blankets provided by the fire department, Jasper and Mary sat in the back of one ambulance with oxygen masks covering their faces. Harry and Susan were in the other ambulance with black cadaver bags covering theirs.

Despite the heroic efforts of Jasper and Mary, they didn't get to the Broadmoars in time to be spared a carbon-monoxide-poisoning death. Mary was able to describe the symptoms of nausea, confusion, and fatigue to the firemen who immediately tested the air in the home. The carbon monoxide reading was 170 parts per million, which even exposed for a short amount of time, was surely a deadly level. The fire chief told Jasper and Mary they were lucky to be alive.

The EMT caring for them insisted they be taken to the hospital for observation. He explained that it would take ten to twenty-four hours for all the carbon monoxide in their bodies to be replaced with oxygen. Jasper and Mary exchanged glances. *Twenty-four hours? We don't have twenty-four hours!*

Officer Jancy was one of the police detectives that responded to this emergency call. He was awakened by the scanner at his home and recalled that Jasper and Mary said that was where they would be staying. He got dressed and hurried to the B&B.

After Officer Jancy got the details from the fire chief and the EMT at the ambulance holding the Broadmoars, he approached Jasper and Mary.

Very weak and still coughing, Jasper nodded a hello as he shook the officer's hand. Jancy turned to Mary. "So what happened here tonight?"

"I felt nauseous and weak. It took me a little while to realize it wasn't just a case of my dinner not sitting well. I didn't smell anything. The inside of the house was quiet, and I didn't see anything out of the ordinary outside." Mary's voice trailed off a little before continuing, "I am so sorry we didn't reach Harry and Susan in time. What did the fire chief have to say?"

"The preliminary inspection confirmed a break in a seal along the furnace exhaust. That would explain the carbon monoxide leaking into the house. With the Broadmoars gone, the chief will do some more investigating tomorrow: checking local furnace repair companies, looking through paperwork, etc. Anything that can shed light on whether they were aware of any furnace troubles. It might just be a case of an old house with an old furnace."

"Maybe," Mary muttered. "Did you hear that Officer Winston located Tricia's car?"

"No, I haven't checked in with anyone yet. I'm technically not on duty, but when I heard the emergency call come over the scanner, I had to check on you two. Where did they find the car?"

As Mary was filling Officer Jancy in on what little she and Jasper had learned the night before, Jasper's phone rang.

"Cheryl." Jasper removed the oxygen mask and walked away, still wrapped in a blanket, to finish his conversation.

"Oh, Jasper, I didn't wake you, did I? I got your message. Patricia's car was found at the train station?" Cheryl said in a confused tone.

Jasper coughed once, then cleared his throat before responding. "Cheryl, that's right, but first, I need to give you some very bad news."

"Oh no, I am starting to get used to that, Jasper," Cheryl said, feebly trying to inject a little bit of lightheartedness.

"Cheryl, the Broadmoars are dead."

"What!" Cheryl exclaimed. "How?"

"Suspected carbon monoxide poisoning. The furnace had a broken seal in the exhaust. Mary and I are lucky to be alive."

"Oh my god, Jasper! This is awful! Harry and Susan were such wonderful people." Cheryl choked backed tears, continuing, "They were so happy. The B&B was closed up for the season, and they were going on a three-week cruise next month. Everyone down at the Lighthouse Preservation Society is going to be devastated. I'll call the secretary to get the word out. Is that Jim Bonner or Greg Farley? Oh my god! They had a grandson due this spring. I need to call their daughter! I can't believe this." Full-blown tears flowed now.

After a moment or two, Cheryl composed herself. "How did you and Mary escape?"

Jasper told her how Mary had saved his life and nearly saved the Broadmoars as well. Then, he said, "Mary and I will hopefully be able to get back inside and gather our things. We want to come back out to the farm. Is Sterling there?"

"I'll check," and then after a moment, she said, "Yeah, Jasper, I see his truck down the way. I'll put on some coffee and cook up some eggs and toast. See you when you get here... Oh my god, I can't believe Harry and Susan are gone. I imagine Harold Jr will take care of the arrangements. Somebody has to tell Pastor Jack down at the First Baptist on Union... I'll have to cook up a couple of meals to take down there. Probably some chicken and pasta and a bunch of potatoes—"

Jasper cut the rambling Cheryl off, "Cheryl, we'll be here a little while longer. We will see you around eight. I am sorry about the Broadmoars."

Mary used her celebrity and sway with Officer Jancy to convince him to let her and Jasper reenter the house. They were both fitted with portable oxygen tanks and escorted back in by a couple of members of the fire department. It took them about twenty minutes to dress and pack, and by seven thirty, they were thanking all the first responders and departing for UBB. Officer Jancy indicated they would process Trish's car for fingerprints, blood, and DNA. He said he would be in contact when they were finished, and Jasper could pick up the car.

Jasper and Mary were very quiet on the ride to UBB, lost in their own respective thoughts. All the excitement at the B&B and the unfortunate end of life for the Broadmoars had temporarily distracted them from thinking about Trish, but now, as they got farther from that scene, the fears and realizations from the prior evening flooded back.

"Jasper, do you think Sterling was being completely honest with you?" Mary finally broke the silence as she carefully navigated the snow-covered roads.

"Of course, I do. What are you even suggesting, Mary?"

"Jammers, it is my job to consider all possibilities. Sometimes, you have to take your heart out of the equation. You can't let your emotions or personal relationships cloud over the clues."

"Sterling and Trish have been friends their entire lives. He's the nicest guy I have ever known. If he told me Tricia was headed back to Manhattan, then Tricia was headed back to Manhattan," Jasper said with just a hint of hesitation.

With that, they made the turn up the driveway and slowly approached the large *M* that centered the security gate. Cheryl must have been looking out, and the gate began to swing open.

When Cheryl greeted them at the front door, her eyes were red, and tissues were spilling from the pockets of her bathrobe. She was disheveled from head to toe and appeared to be exhausted. She led them back to the kitchen where she had coffee, sausage, and eggs waiting.

As they got seated, Cheryl finally broke the silence. "I am so very thankful that you two were able to get out of the house. It sounds like you were just moments away from suffering the same fate as Harry and Susan."

"Yeah, I am trying not to think about it," Jasper responded.

"Cheryl, did you get Jasper's message? Tricia's car was found at the train station. Do you have any idea why this would be?" Mary asked, reaching for the creamer.

"I did get that message and admit that is very strange. She didn't make any mention of a train when I spoke with her, but I remind you, our last conversation was not a friendly one." Cheryl went on, "She was so unhappy, Jasper. Maybe she just wants to get away from both of us for a while?"

"It doesn't make any sense, Cheryl. She had all that work done on the car. She was planning on a long drive, not a quick jaunt to the train station. Something is seriously wrong!" Jasper worried as he played with his eggs. He couldn't eat. He was still nauseous from the carbon monoxide he inhaled.

The three of them continued to work through the possibilities and couldn't come up with any logical explanation that didn't place Trish in a dangerous situation. All three of them were feeling anxious. It was agreed they needed to get down to the guesthouse to see Sterling.

As Cheryl was putting away the last of the breakfast dishes, Jasper asked, "Cheryl, are you coming to see Sterling with us?"

"No. I think I need to head to church a little early to fill Pastor Jack in on the Broadmoars' unfortunate demise. The parishioners will certainly be in shock once the news spreads through town. Please let me know what Sterling tells you or if you hear anything from the police. Or better yet, if you find Tricia."

*****

Ring. Voice mail. Tricia's phone was still shut off.

CHAPTER 16

December 23, 2018, 9:00 AM

Jasper and Mary thanked Cheryl for breakfast and headed down to the guesthouse to talk to Sterling.

Unbreakable Bonds was beautiful this Sunday morning. Fresh snow had blanketed the lands overnight, and everything looked so peaceful. But to Jasper and Mary, there was nothing serene about it. They had just narrowly escaped death due to carbon monoxide poisoning, there was no sign of Tricia although her car was found oddly at the local train station, and their friend Sterling seemed to hold some of the missing pieces.

"Why did Sterling say Tricia was getting ready for a long drive if she was really taking a train somewhere?" Mary asked Jasper even though she knew he didn't know the answer.

"I wonder if she told him where she was really going, and he is just covering for her," she continued.

"Covering for her from what?" Jasper snapped back. All this stress was wearing Jasper down. It had been a week since he saw his wife, and he wasn't fully recovered from the oxygen depletion his body had just experienced.

"Sorry, Jammers. I'm a PI, remember? You asked for my help, and I'm trying to give it. It's my nature to ask questions."

Jasper let the conversation die as they walked onto the porch of the guesthouse.

Why is this still called the guesthouse? This was the Shapiro home even before Sterling was born!

Jasper knocked as Mary nosily tried to look through the window, but the curtains were drawn, and her curiosity would have to wait.

Jasper knocked again louder.

"His truck is still here. There are no footprints leading to the barn. He has to be here."

This time, Mary knocked.

"Sterling!" she yelled. "It's Mary and Jasper. We need to talk." She jiggled the doorknob, but it wouldn't turn.

"I'll check around back," Jasper said as he was already skipping the last step and jumping in the snow.

Mary nervously peered again through the window as if hoping the curtain had moved since the last time she looked. It hadn't. She put her ear to the glass but heard nothing from inside.

Jasper returned to Mary and announced he couldn't get in the back either, and he couldn't see lights on through the kitchen window. The house was still.

"I'm breaking in, Mary." And with that, Jasper pulled his coat sleeve over his fist and punched the glass of the front door. He punched three more times before shattering it enough to push his hand all the way in to reach the lock from the inside.

As the door swung open, Mary screamed, "Sterling!"

*****

Without even thinking, Jasper ran to his friend just hanging there.

Pushing up on Sterling's legs, he cried out, "Sterling! No! Oh my god! Sterling! No, buddy! No!" He called to Mary, "Mary, help! Hold him up! I need to get him down!"

Mary just looked at Jasper. Her eyes were pained, her lips pursed as if ready to cry.

Jasper shouted, "Mary, what are you doing? Get over here! Hurry! Help me! We can't let him die!"

Mary's voice was weak. "It's too late, Jammers. He's dead. He has been dead for a while."

In Mary's time as a police officer, she had the unfortunate experience of seeing people in various stages after death. In that time, she had seen two suicide hanging victims. She first recognized the swelling of Sterling's feet. The longer a body hangs, the longer gravity has to pull fluids downward. Her second clue was the depth of the rope as it furrowed into Sterling's neck over time as the skin around it began the decaying process.

"We can't leave him like this, Mary! Help me!"

But Mary turned away as she pulled her phone from her jacket pocket and dialed 911—for the second time in six hours.

*****

Dispatch had put Mary through to Officer Jancy's cell phone after sending an ambulance and other officers. "Hello, Officer Jancy. You need to get to UBB right away. Jasper and I just found Sterling dead in the guesthouse… He hanged himself… No, other than Jasper breaking a small window pane of the front door and touching Sterling's legs in an attempt to get him down, we've touched nothing… We will… See you soon."

As Mary was having her conversation with Officer Jancy, Jasper called Cheryl. She didn't answer, and he couldn't bring himself to say anything more in the voice mail than, "Cheryl, you need to call me right away."

"Jasper, Officer Jancy said to wait outside until police get here." Puzzled to find Jasper sitting on the edge of the couch looking at a laptop on the coffee table, Mary asked, "What are you doing? You can't touch anything!"

"Mary, you need to come see this."

*****

Dear Mom,
We may not share the same blood, but you
are my mother. I have felt your love and devotion
from my earliest memories. You have always been
so kind to me…given me so many opportunities.
I have disappointed you. Please forgive me.
Love, Your Sterling

*****

The next five minutes felt like five hours as Jasper and Mary paced in the driveway outside the guesthouse waiting for help to arrive. The paramedics arrived first. A quick survey of Sterling's condition confirmed what Mary had detected: this was not a mission in hopes of saving a life.

The responding police officers stopped to get some preliminary details from Jasper and Mary, then headed into the house. Officer Jancy was next on the scene.

"We have to stop meeting like this, Mary. Jasper, how are you feeling?"

"I've been better. Six hours ago, I was pulling a dead couple from their home, and just now, I found my friend dangling from the ceiling."

Jasper's glare pierced through Officer Jancy. It's not that he had anything against the officer; he was just tired. Tired of searching, tired of one tragedy after another, tired of not having Trish by his side.

Mary piped in, "We told the first responding officers about the suicide note on the laptop. Other than that, we really have no more information to offer. We had no contact with Sterling since yesterday afternoon…about an hour or so before we came and saw you at the police station. Jasper has already tried to contact Cheryl Maxwell but hasn't gotten through yet."

"Thanks, Mary. We definitely need to speak with Ms. Maxwell." Officer Jancy looked around the grounds. He spotted the footprints in the snow on the side of the house. "Did you make these, or were they here when you arrived?"

"Jasper made those when he went around back trying to get… to get Sterling's attention when we first arrived." Mary couldn't help her crackling voice. She realized that she had been in investigation mode, and the sadness of Sterling's death hadn't quite kicked in yet.

Officer Jancy put a sympathetic hand on Mary's shoulder. "I'll be back to check on you soon. Just hang tight." He offered a smile and a nod and then turned to make his way inside.

Jasper had made his way over to Sterling's old farm truck. Sitting on the bumper, hunched over with his head in his hands, Mary approached him.

"Jammers, I'm so sorry about Sterling."

"Thanks, Mary. But he was just as much your friend as he was mine. We both lost someone special." He reached out for Mary's hand and led her to sit beside him. They embraced and finally cried. They shared the release of all the emotion of the last couple of days. Neither could let go. Neither wanted to.

*****

After some time, they composed themselves and tried to piece it all together. Jasper played the note through in his head.

"Mary, what did Sterling mean by disappointing Cheryl? What bad things has he done?" Trying to fight back the words, he continued, "Do you think he has done something to Trish?"

"Oh, Jasper. Something just isn't adding up that's for sure. I felt something odd last night after we learned about Trish's car at the train station. I guess I was suspecting Sterling was involved but just didn't want to admit it. But now…now…," Mary still couldn't verbalize what her mind was processing. She sat there for a minute to run through the checklist in her mind.

Fact: Cheryl said she and Tricia argued. Cheryl wanted Trish to return to Jasper.

Fact: Sterling said he had Trish's car serviced before she started her drive home to Manhattan.

Fact: Trish did not arrive in Manhattan that night, but rather, her car was found parked in the long-term parking lot of the train station.

Fact: Sterling told Jasper he knew about their marital problems, which means Tricia had shared a lot while on this visit.

Fact: Sterling is dead. Suicide. Said he did bad things.

"Mary, Mary, are you listening?"

Snapping out of her thoughts, Mary said, "Sorry, Jasper. What did you say?"

"I asked you if Officer Jancy had mentioned anything about when he could expect the results of Tricia's car inspection."

"No. He didn't mention how long it would take. Let's ask him. Here he comes now."

Officer Jancy walked toward the two of them carrying something in a plastic evidence bag. It was Sterling's cell phone.

"You need to see this. What do you make of it?" Officer Jancy said as he held up the baggie with a picture showing on the screen.

"That's Tricia!" exclaimed Jasper as he grabbed the evidence from Jancy's hand.

Mary leaned in close to see what Jasper was looking at. Right there, on Sterling's phone was a picture of Tricia…in a hospital bed… with birthday balloons.

"This was just taken yesterday," Jasper said matter-of-factly. "Sterling was with Trish yesterday!" Jasper's heart starting pounding hard in his chest, and his hands began to shake.

Mary took the phone from Jasper to get a closer look, and swiping her fingers on the screen through the plastic evidence bag, she zoomed in and focused on something in the background.

"Jasper, do you recognize this place?" Mary asked as she moved the phone closer to Jasper.

Jasper jumped up. "Yes, oh my god. Mary, we have to get to Tricia, NOW! Officer Jancy, would you mind coming with us?"

CHAPTER 17

December 23, 2018, 11:00 AM

Westfield Memorial Hospital was a twelve-minute drive from Unbreakable Bonds. With Officer Jancy's police-siren escort, it took them eight.

Mary swerved into the parking spot beside the police cruiser and barely had time to put the car in park before Jasper had exited, leaving the passenger door ajar. Mary and Officer Jancy raced after him. At the reception desk in the emergency room, Jasper asked if Tricia Merwood was a patient at the hospital.

"I don't see anyone by that name, sir," the receptionist answered calmly.

Mary moved from behind Jasper and held up her phone. She had taken a picture of the photo of Tricia from Sterling's phone that had been retained by the police. "Was this photo taken here at the hospital?"

"Let me see," the middle-aged woman said as she took the phone from Mary and adjusted her bifocals to get a better look. "Yes. This looks like it was taken from the third floor overlooking the Westfield Memorial Garden."

"Is the woman in this picture a patient here?" demanded Jasper.

"Sir, I am not privy to every patient in this hospital," was the receptionist's still calm response until Officer Jancy made his way to the desk, flashing his detective badge, and repeating the question.

The receptionist sat a little straighter in her seat, cleared her throat, and apologized to the officer.

"That picture does look like it was taken here, and the woman in the picture obviously looks like a patient, but there is no Tricia Merwood registered."

"Try Tricia Maxwell," blurted Jasper.

The receptionist typed in the name, smiled, and said, "There she is. Tricia Maxwell. Room 307. That's in the psychiatric ward."

Jasper and Mary exchanged puzzled looks. *The psych ward?*

"How do we get there?" Officer Jancy asked.

"Take the elevators to three, hang a left, go straight through the double doors, and then turn right toward the security desk. You'll need to get permission to enter," the receptionist's voice got louder so the three could hear her as they had already begun hurrying down the corridor. "The elevator bank is just around the—" she didn't bother to finish because they were already out of sight.

But then, Officer Jancy appeared from around the corner, gave a wave, and hollered to the receptionist, "Thanks for the assist, ma'am."

Jasper, Mary, and Officer Jancy followed the instructions, and as they made the right turn after passing through the double doors, Jasper stopped dead in his tracks.

Up ahead, standing with a nurse at the security desk was Cheryl Maxwell.

"Cheryl? Cheryl!" Jasper called out. "What are you doing here? Do you know that Tricia is here?" Jasper was completely lost and bewildered. They had just figured out from the picture on Sterling's phone that Tricia had been at this hospital the day before. How did Cheryl know? Why was she here?

"Jasper…Mary," stuttered Cheryl as she turned around, clearly surprised to see Officer Jancy was also with them. After a deep breath, she answered, "Yes, Jasper, Tricia is here, and she doesn't want to see you."

"Doesn't want to see me? What is going on? Why is she in this psych ward?" Jasper was waving his arms, and his voice was rising with every word.

"Sir, please keep your voice down. We don't want to disturb the patients," scolded the nurse standing with Cheryl.

After giving the nurse a quick glare, Jasper turned to Cheryl and deliberately asked again a few decibels lower, "Why is Tricia here, and why doesn't she want to see me?"

"Jasper, you are the reason she is here. You put her here, and now, you need to leave us alone."

"She is my wife! You have lied to me for days! You knew how worried I have been, yet you lied to me! Sterling lied to me. I sat around your breakfast table this morning, and I feared my wife was dead, and you said nothing. Nothing! How could you? You probably also knew that Sterling was dead, yet you let me find him like that!"

"Sterling is dead? What are you talking about, Jasper?"

"Take me to my wife, Cheryl! Now!"

"What do you mean Sterling is dead? What did you do to Sterling?"

Mary stepped in between Jasper and Cheryl.

"Cheryl, I am sorry to inform you that Sterling took his own life…presumably sometime overnight. He left you a note."

Cheryl wiped away a tear, took a deep breath, and addressed the issue at hand.

"Jasper, I brought her here for her own good. She was upset when I told her she should go back to you and work things out. She indicated that she would rather kill herself than see you again." She paused to watch Jasper's shocked reaction to what she had just said and then continued. "I had to go to the Wine America policy meeting, and I didn't trust her at the farmhouse alone. I would have discharged her yesterday, and Sterling, Trish, and I would have celebrated her birthday…if you hadn't showed up. You always ruin everything, Jasper.

"Just go home. Go back to your luxurious Manhattan apartment and your pampered life and leave us alone!"

Jasper ignored Cheryl and focused on the nurse. "Take me to my wife, NOW!" Jasper screamed, and the nurse jumped back in slight fear.

Officer Jancy placed a hand on Jasper's shoulder and raised his other hand to the nurse as if to gesture that he had everything under control.

"Ma'am, my name is Officer Curtis Jancy, and I request that you take us to Tricia Maxwell's room."

"Tricia MERWOOD," emphasized Jasper.

Jasper and Cheryl exchanged glares. "Fine, Jasper, go. You win this round, but this fight isn't over. Not by a long shot!" Cheryl threw the discharge papers in Jasper's face and headed toward the double doors that led back to the elevators. "Apparently, I have to go home and bury my son!"

Tears ran down Cheryl's cheeks as she boarded the elevator.

The nurse pushed the button to unlock the doors to the patient wing. Jasper, Mary, and Officer Jancy found the sign indicating the hallway for rooms 300–320 and headed to see Trish.

*****

Mary hung back as Jasper rushed ahead to room 307. So many emotions were rushing through her at this very moment. On one hand, she was elated that her friend was found safe, but on the other, she was not prepared to witness the happy reunion that was about to take place. She silently reprimanded herself for agreeing to take this trip with him. *How am I ever going to push Jasper Merwood out of my mind and move on with my life?*

As Jasper approached the door, he slowed and tried to compose himself. He wasn't sure what state he would find Tricia in, and he didn't want to startle her. He was not completely successful as Tricia jolted up in the bed, causing the semideflated birthday balloons to shiver.

Jasper could not hide the relief and joy he felt seeing Tricia. His whole body shook, and tears flowed freely as all the tension and fear of the past week exited him. He ran to Tricia and held her tight.

"Oh my god, Trish, you don't know how happy I am to see you! I've missed you so badly. I tried calling you so many times. I wasn't sure if you were dead or alive. I didn't know where you were. I needed to know you were okay. Are you okay?" he asked, not wanting to pull back from the embrace. Finally, he released and looked at her.

"They took my phone," was Tricia's subdued response. A solitary tear rolled down her cheek.

Jasper's own excitement impeded him from noticing Tricia's muted reaction.

He continued effusively, "Trish, I have been such a jerk. I am so sorry. No more, I promise. I love you so much. I swear I will give you…give us…my full attention. We will go to movies and dinners and weekends away. I will even watch that show *That Is Us* or *That Was Us* or whatever it is." Jasper chuckled gleefully. "No more feeling sorry for myself."

He pulled her close again.

"I want us to start a family. We are going to be great parents. I can picture it already: I will coach the soccer team, and you will bake the brownies for the postgame snack. Life is going to be great! Because I will have you, and we will be together forever!" Jasper brought his face to hers, but instead of kissing, he noticed Trish was now in full tears…and not happy ones.

"Tricia?"

"Jasper," Tricia began, voice cracking, barely above a whisper, "I have learned something…something…"

She fell deeper into Jasper's arms. He held her tight.

"Trish, you can tell me anything. What's wrong?" Jasper pleaded, not really sure if he wanted to hear what she was trying to say or not.

"Jasper," Trish started again through her tears. "We…"

CHAPTER 18

December 23, 2018, 11:15 AM

Tricia was startled when she saw her old college friend Mary Sintag and Officer Curtis Jancy, the brother of a boy she dated in high school, walk into the room.

"What's going on? What are you two doing here?" Tricia wiped tears from her eyes as she pulled the bedsheets closer to her neck.

"Hi, Tricia, it's been too long. I am so happy that you are safe," responded Mary first as she leaned over to give her friend a hug.

Officer Jancy settled at the foot of the bed and nodded a hello. Tricia looked confused and darted glances between her three visitors. "What is going on?"

Jasper took Tricia's hand.

"Trish, we're hoping you can tell us. What were you just about to tell me?"

Tricia started crying again and just shook her head no.

"Trish, please, please, help me understand what is happening," Jasper begged.

She took a deep breath, looked at Mary, Officer Jancy, and finally settled her gaze on Jasper.

"Oh, Jasper, our world is falling apart. When my mom called and urged me to come to Westfield, I had no idea how it would change our lives."

Jasper was puzzled but encouraged her to continue.

"Jasper, you and I are related. My father is your father too." Tricia was sobbing through the words. Jasper just stared at her.

"What are you talking about, Trish? This is nonsense!"

"I'm so sorry, Jasper. My mom said she just found out. She needed to get me away from you so she could tell me. I'm a mess. I can't think straight. I must have had a nervous breakdown, and that's why Mom brought me here. I didn't know how to tell you, Jasper. What are we going to do?"

Officer Jancy and Mary looked at each other in disbelief. But something in Mary caused her to blurt out, "Did Sterling know?"

Caught off guard at such a question, Tricia glared at Mary and answered, "I...I don't think so. I didn't tell him. And he didn't say anything to me about it." Tricia noticed the awkward glances between Jasper and Mary and continued, "What does Sterling have to do with this?"

Jasper, still dazed and bewildered, suddenly snapped back to reality.

"Oh, Trish, there's something I need to tell you. Mary and Officer Jancy, would you mind giving us some privacy?"

Mary squeezed Tricia's shoulder and, without saying a word, left the room with Jancy.

*****

"What do you make of that, Mary?" Officer Jancy asked as soon as the room door was closed behind them.

Mary shook her head in disbelief.

"Oh my god, I have no clue. Everything is cloudy, and I mean everything." Mary closed her eyes and rubbed her temples. "Jancy, we're looking at this all wrong." And with that, Mary started pacing the hallway as she struggled to make sense of the recent events.

"First, if Cheryl just found out that Jasper and Tricia are half siblings," again a head shake as this soaked in, she said, "HOW did she find out?

"Second, I know we didn't get any details from Tricia just now, but how and why did Cheryl get Tricia here...in the psych ward... cutting off all communication with Jasper? Why keep him uninformed? Furthermore, she had every opportunity the last couple of days to tell us, and she didn't.

"Third, what did Sterling know? What did Sterling do? Based on the photo in his phone, he was with Trish yesterday here at the hospital for her birthday. Then, he hanged himself last night after writing a letter to Cheryl apologizing for disappointing her. How did he disappoint her? Something is not adding up for me."

Officer Jancy watched Mary pace up and down the hallway.

Just then, Mary spun around and asked, "Are the police still at Sterling's house? Tell them to treat it like a crime scene. Jancy, we need a full autopsy on Sterling. This wasn't a suicide."

PART 2

CHAPTER 19

Cheryl

Cheryl Winters was born in the dead of winter in Jamestown, New York. Her parents, Samuel and Grace, made the trek north to Chautauqua Medical Center at approximately three thirty on that Sunday morning. Samuel had to clear roughly five inches of snow and a thick layer of ice off his beat-up old Ford pickup while Grace sat in the passenger seat, moaning in pain every few minutes or so, at the start of another contraction. Cheryl had arrived a week and a half early, catching her parents off guard. Samuel and Grace were exhausted from a sleepless evening followed by the perilous drive in the snowstorm, but none of the staff or visitors to the hospital could tell. They were overjoyed. They were ecstatic. They could not conceal their excitement.

The Winters were in their early forties when they met and had tried fruitlessly for more than five years to conceive a child. They had all but given up hope, and the constant failure and disappointment had, on several occasions, nearly caused the marriage to fall apart. Neither could remember ever being happier than on that day when Dr. Cirelli announced that Grace was pregnant. It was the answer to a million prayers. Never happier, that is, until that Sunday when a beautiful, healthy Cheryl was placed in Grace's arms.

Sam and Grace had always gotten by on modest means; neither had a strong education. They lived in a tiny two-bedroom shack located on New York State Route 60. Its wooden clapboard siding showed the wear of many years of passing truck traffic. Sam worked a line job in the Purina plant thirty-five miles north in Dunkirk, and Grace bounced around from job to job. But once Cheryl entered their lives, they were determined to make sure she didn't want for anything.

In the first few years after Cheryl's birth, Sam would pick up extra shifts and overtime pay at every opportunity. Grace would work the dinner shift at Jackson's Diner, and on the weekends, she manned a toll booth on Interstate 90, just a few miles north of the Pennsylvania border.

While they both worked hard, they also made sure that one of them was always around, doting and loving on Cheryl. On those occasions that the three of them were able to spend time together, they often went on long drives through the Western New York countryside. Cheryl loved the animals. She would scream out "cows" or "sheep" at every passing farm, but her favorite animal was, without a doubt, the horses.

Sam's hard work paid off, and shortly before Cheryl's fifth birthday, he was promoted to production manager and received a substantial pay increase. The next weekend, the Winters family was on one of their drives as they came upon Unbreakable Bonds on Route 20 in Westfield. They spotted a couple of horses out feeding, and on Cheryl's request, Sam slowed and made the turn onto the estate grounds. As Cheryl admired the beautiful creatures, Grace noted the sign out front offering rides and riding lessons. They agreed, with their newfound fortune, that this would be a wonderful way to celebrate and made their way up toward the main building.

Mr. Maxwell himself met the Winters at the admissions office and led them back to the stables. Cheryl was so excited to be this close. She could not contain her glee as she ran toward a majestic brown beauty eating from the food trough. She put her hand out, and the horse brushed it with her nose and gave out a loud neigh. Cheryl squealed with joy.

Mr. Maxwell fumbled around for the waiver forms and the riding lesson information pamphlets. He explained that his wife had recently passed, and she had handled all the "darn paperwork." He had hired a local teenager, but he had called off that morning with a headache. "Must have had an entertaining evening."

Eventually, Samuel ended up paying for an introductory lesson for Cheryl. A stable hand led them to the corral, and Cheryl was introduced to a young filly named Sandy. For the next hour, Cheryl and Sandy became acquainted and made several laps around the perimeter of the corral. The instructor was absolutely amazed at how quickly Cheryl took to riding. She was a natural, belting out the commands and encouraging Sandy to do as she desired. Horse and rider seemed to have an innate bond. The others working nearby were in awe of five-year-old Cheryl, and word quickly got back to Mr. Maxwell who made his way out to watch the talented little girl. He was equally impressed.

When the lesson was completed, Cheryl raced over to her mom and dad, giving them both big hugs and thanking them for the best day of her life. The instructor explained to Sam and Grace just how good Cheryl was, and that she would be honored to be able to continue lessons with her. Sam's eyes glanced down at the pricing information in his hand, swallowing hard. Then, he looked at his daughter's eyes and her smile. Of course, he told the instructor, of course, they would continue.

From that point forward, Cheryl grew up in two worlds. At home, she watched her parents struggle for everything they had, which wasn't much. They were always working or worrying or fighting. It was always stressful. They rarely found time to relax or enjoy life. Except, of course, when it came to her.

The Maxwells, on the other hand, had everything they could possibly want. They too worked hard, but life was easy. Life was fun.

Cheryl loved her parents and was grateful for everything they provided her, but she did not want that life. She decided at a very young age that she was going to have the lifestyle of the Maxwells, and that she would do whatever was required to make that happen.

*****

As the years passed, Cheryl's talent soared. She was special, and she knew it. So did everyone else down at UBB. They showed her talents off annually at the Chautauqua County Fair and various other community farm events. Eventually, she was performing in front of crowds all over the tri-state area.

The stables at UBB benefitted greatly. There were waiting lists for boarding at the stables as well as for riding lessons. Cheryl's notoriety and the success of the stables produced residual benefits for the other Maxwell businesses including the winery. Winery visitation and sales took off, and, in fact, Unbreakable Bonds became the number one most visited winery along the Lake Erie Wine Trail.

Cheryl was determined and laser focused. She spent every available minute working at her craft. She knew this was her path to fame and fortune and the life that she craved. As she entered her high school years, she became the lead riding instructor. In exchange, the Maxwells offered her free room and board and unlimited access to the horses and the stables. They also paid for tutors, and Cheryl was able to spend most of her day at the farm.

The Maxwells charged top dollar for Cheryl's lessons, and the demand remained high season after season. Mr. Maxwell was quite content with everything, but Cheryl wanted more.

Cheryl did all the research and pushed Mr. Maxwell to submit an application to the United States Equestrian Federation (USEF) for the stables at Unbreakable Bonds to be an Elite Training Center. They qualified for such title with Cheryl's recent classification as a developing rider, a designation she achieved because of her success in competitions.

With this certification, the stables at UBB became a regional destination for aspiring riders, well beyond Western New York. Cheryl herself had been very successful in USEF-sanctioned championships. She was well on her way toward qualifying for the 1984

Olympics, and the local media was taking notice. One writer opined that they should rename the training center as the Cheryl Winters Stables at Unbreakable Bonds, and Cheryl took notice.

Cheryl appreciated Mr. Maxwell and the opportunity he had provided her. But while he had been accommodating and kind, and in many ways a second father, Cheryl never felt he fully recognized her singular importance to the farm. On a couple of occasions when she mentioned increased compensation or higher stature within the company, he had chuckled or put her off, never taking her seriously.

Shortly after the reporter made his "Cheryl Winters Stables" comment, Cheryl asked for a serious sit-down at the house with Mr. Maxwell. Cheryl laid it all out on the table. She was the biggest reason for his success, and it was time that she was given her just rewards. The naming of the stables would be a great start.

Mr. Maxwell laughed and, in a condescending tone, let Cheryl know that the name change would not be considered. He told her he was grateful for what she had done for the farm, but then, he reminded her that everything she had was a direct result of her association with UBB, and she should be equally grateful. He felt she had become quite arrogant over the years. With that, Mr. Maxwell guided her to the door. The meeting was over. As he swung it open, he decreed, "This business is a Maxwell family operation and will always remain so. The only name that will ever reside on any of the buildings on this property will be Maxwell."

As he finished, Cheryl saw Rex Maxwell heading out the front door. She thought about Mr. Maxwell's last words and then shouted "Hey, Rex, wait up a second," and followed him out the door.

CHAPTER 20

Summer 1984

"Of course, I will marry you, Rex! Oh, sweetie, this ring is so beautiful. How could things be any better?"

The other patrons in Fabrizio's Italian restaurant were on their feet applauding. Several lined up to give me a hug and slap Rex on the back to tell us how happy they were and proud of the Maxwell family.

As Rex and I made our way down Main Street to the car, horns were honking, and people were shouting congratulations on the Olympic medals. I waved back, flashing my new engagement ring, and soaked in all the adulation. I am the town of Westfield's hero, and I love it! And now, I will be the wife of the only heir to the Maxwell fortune.

I suspected the controlling Mr. Maxwell would not be thrilled to hear the news of our engagement, and a few days later, the suspicion was confirmed when I overheard a conversation between Rex and his father.

"But, Dad, you don't know her like I do."

"Rex, trust me, I know Cheryl Winters. For one thing, she has let her riding success go to her head. Don't get me wrong. I saw greatness in her when she was young, and I still see an extremely talented equestrian. Heck, the whole world sees that with all her Olympic medals. But there's something more to her, Rex, that just doesn't sit well with me. This is **our** family business." Mr. Maxwell came out from behind his desk, sat on the edge in front of Rex, and continued, "I know she deserves our respect and affection, but she thinks she owns this corporation just because she's a great rider. There's so much more to this business than just the stables. She can't take credit for our decades of success just because of a few good riding years. You understand, don't you, son?"

"Dad, just let Cheryl have this moment in the spotlight. Everything will settle down soon, and you'll love having her as your daughter-in-law."

"I hope you are planning on letting things 'settle down' before you actually marry her then. You don't have my blessing yet." Mr. Maxwell turned and walked out of the office, mumbling as he went, "I hope you're considering a prenup!"

*****

That fall, Mr. Maxwell was systematically harvesting the corn in field C-1, the most northwest quadrant of the farmlands. This section of the field bordered the road and an adjacent horse trail. Snow and I came up from the road and started down the trail, passing Mr. Maxwell. He waved at me as I went by; I waved back.

Go ahead and wave, you fool. You wave hello, I wave goodbye.

A few moments later, I circled back around, frantically waving for Mr. Maxwell to stop. He put the harvester in neutral and jumped down.

"What is it, Cheryl? What is wrong?"

"Up ahead, in the corn…it's a fawn, and I think he's injured."

As Mr. Maxwell took a couple of steps in the direction I was pointing, I pulled the shovel from the saddlebag and cracked him at the base of his skull. He was dead before he hit the ground.

I quickly dismounted Snow and dragged Mr. Maxwell's lifeless body through the corn in front of the harvester. The ungodly sound of a body being shredded would have brought most to their knees, but it was a beautiful sound to me. It was the sound of me finally getting my just reward.

Of course, this isn't what I planned on doing. It was an impulse made when the opportunity presented itself. It was a believable accident, but still, I had to play my hand with caution.

I led the machine straight ahead into the trees at the edge of the field until it came to a natural stop. I jumped on Snow and rode back toward the stables, speeding my breathing and planning my dialogue.

"Help, help! Anyone, I need your help!" I frantically screamed as I got closer to the barn. Some workers came running, and I told them I thought Mr. Maxwell was in danger. "I saw the corn harvester against some trees, and Mr. Maxwell was nowhere to be found." I watched as the crew rode out to help their beloved boss.

Sorry, Mr. Maxwell, it didn't have to be like this, but you left me no choice. Your unfortunate demise will be passed off as a freak accident, and I will be there to console your son. Don't worry, we'll remember you fondly at the wedding.

CHAPTER 21

Present Time

Oh, and we did remember you. I made sure there was a memorial table with pictures and cards and special tokens from your past. In fact, your portrait still hangs above the walnut mantel that you built, in the house that you built, on the farm that you started. The mantel, the house, the farm that you did not want me to have. Well, it's all mine now, Mr. Maxwell. It's all mine now.

Cheryl Maxwell sat in silence, sipping a glass of bourbon, and staring blankly at the unlit fireplace in the living room. The events at the hospital this morning had not gone as planned. None of the last few days had gone as planned.

Cheryl was holding the gun that had belonged to her late husband, Rex. It was a relic that she had only recently become aware of. Cheryl's cell phone rang. It was Jasper…probably calling from the hospital. She wasn't ready for that conversation yet, so she put the phone in her pocket.

Don't worry, Jasper, we will talk soon.

She grabbed her drink and made her way toward the office. Passing the picture of Snow brought another wave of sadness through her. She touched the gun in her waistband and thought about another day of monumental change.

CHAPTER 22

Spring–Summer 1992

I was excited about my plans for the day. After a workout with Snow, Rebecca and I were going to head into town with Tricia for her Easter pictures and have lunch.

I was almost to the stables when I realized I forgot my goggles back at the main house. When I returned, I overheard Rex on the phone in the office just off the kitchen.

"I know, Paige. I need to figure this out. I miss you too. I think about you all the time... I know we have been through a lot, and you have been more than patient with me... Please don't worry, my darling. Just give me a little more time to figure out how to make this work as painlessly for Cheryl as possible... Yes, I promise I will tell her soon... I love you too..."

I staggered, catching myself on the kitchen table, feeling like I had been hit by a sledgehammer. I struggled to compose myself, grabbed the goggles, and started back down to the stables. I was in a trance. My mind had gone blank. My head and the world around me had gone mute.

"Good morning, Cheryl. Snow is ready to work. Aren't you, girl?"

Had Roger said something? I thought he may have, so I gave him a nod.

Acting from habit alone, I greeted Snow with a couple of pats and climbed aboard. Instinctively, she guided us out to corral B and neighed loudly to signal she was ready to run the course. All of a sudden, my mind was flooded with confusion and sadness, but mostly with rage.

Rex, you are an imbecile. What have you done? How dare you! You cheating son of a ——! You think you can do this to me?

Snow and I began to circle the course. My mind would not focus on the gates, walls, and other corral obstacles that were in front of us. I could only remain focused on the obstacle that Rex had caused and how I would fix it.

Rex, you are the same fool that your father was before you! You think you can remove me from this farm and this money that I am entitled to? I have made Unbreakable Bonds what it is. I have carried us. You would be floundering without my name, my leadership, my business acumen...

"OH NO! Snow! Not yet!"

Snow misjudged a water gate, landed awkwardly, and threw me into an adjacent brick wall obstacle. Roger had been working nearby and came running. He helped me to a bench and called for stable hands to come quickly and tend to Snow. I didn't want to leave her, but the pain in my shoulder, neck, and back was too much. I had broken my collarbone, and the doctors would put me in a neck brace and arm sling. Poor Snow had suffered an irreparable broken leg and had to be put down. I insisted that I be the one to administer the fatal injection of sodium pentobarbital.

Snow, my dear sweet Snow, I am so sorry that I have to say goodbye. It shouldn't be like this. I shouldn't have to do this. If there was any other way, Snow, you know I would take it. I am so, so sorry. I hate him, Snow. I hate Rex for what he has done. I blame him for this accident. Don't worry, I'll make him pay for this.

*****

I kept what I had learned about Rex and Paige to myself. I knew Rex had to go, but I had to be careful. The thought consumed my every day. I was so devastated over the loss of Snow. In all fairness, Rex felt the devastation too, but he had no clue what really caused Snow to miss that jump. He didn't bring up Paige or a separation for months. He was allowing me time to grieve…and plan my next move. *How sweet of him!*

*****

One morning in July brought everything to a head. While sitting at the breakfast table, Rex was filling me in on his plan for another business trip to California to arrange the sale of UBB wine to a well-known distributor. I couldn't hold back any longer.

"Rex, let's just acknowledge the elephant in the room. I know about Paige. She's joining you while you are in California, isn't she?"

"Cheryl, what are you talking about?" Rex replied nervously.

"Don't play it that way. I've known about your affair for months now. Actually, on the day Snow died, I overheard you on the phone with that tramp. You are the reason I was distracted. You are the reason Snow is dead!"

"Cheryl, I'm sorry. I didn't realize you knew." He couldn't even look at me; he just stared into his coffee mug.

"Well, I do know. And now, I want to know what you are planning on doing about it." I sat back in my chair and folded my hands neatly on my lap.

Rex stood up and went to the counter for the coffee pot. While his back was turned, I emptied a vial of some leftover tranquilizer that I had used on Snow into Rex's mug.

Rex refilled both of our cups and sat down. With a deep sigh, he started, "Cheryl, I never wanted to hurt you…"

"I know, Rex. You wanted this to be as painless for me as possible," I said smugly, recalling Rex's words on the phone that day.

Rex uncomfortably took a long drink of coffee. "Cheryl, we are a great team as far as running this business. But let's be honest, we are not much of a couple anymore. We haven't been for some time. I think it will be best for both of us if we separated."

"Rex, are you suggesting that I leave?"

"I am, Cheryl. Of course, you would take a hefty sum of cash to make sure you are comfortable and get resettled. Also, you can remain in charge of the stable operations," Rex said, trying to sound positive.

"Oh, that would work out well for both of us, wouldn't it? And what about our daughter?"

Rex paused, putting down his mug again after draining the liquid inside.

He started hesitantly, "I think it's best if Trish stays here at the farm where she is familiar and comfortable. Let's face it, Cheryl, you have been very distant since Snow was put down. You hardly spend any time with Tricia. I really think it would be best if she stays with me for a while, and you can focus on getting your life in...in...in order." Rex began to stutter, and he rubbed his forehead.

"Are you okay, Rex? You don't look well."

"I'm not feeling well. I need to lie down."

I took Rex to the couch.

"Lie down over here. So that's your plan, Rex? I leave and you keep Tricia? Well, let me tell you my plan."

Rex looked at me dazed and confused.

"You are going to die...here...on this couch...now. Trish and I will remain on this farm together, and we will enjoy the fortune, which I so richly deserve."

"What's happening to me?"

"You are dying, dear. I poisoned your coffee."

Rex, barely able to keep his eyes open, looked at me, and asked, "Why?"

"Did you really think I would walk away from UBB? Rex, honey, just go to sleep. I will take care of everything as I always have."

*****

Even though Rex was only thirty-six years old, everyone knew he had been under a lot of stress lately with running the farm, stables, and winery. When the paramedics arrived, I told them Rex had been complaining of chest pains but refused to go to the hospital. Instead, he just wanted to rest. The next time I checked on him, he was gone.

I declined an autopsy. Being well-known in a small town afforded me the benefit of people respecting my wishes. He died of a heart attack. Enough said.

CHAPTER 23

Present Time

Cheryl felt agitated remembering the events of the past while also fully aware of the challenges of the present. Jasper was her current challenge. When he found out that he was an heir to the UBB corporation, would he try to take it from her? She would not let that happen no matter what it took to stop him!

She sat in the office chair with her third glass of bourbon and began to formulate a plan in her mind:

1. Call the hospital and find out when Trish is set to be discharged.
2. Park the car several blocks away in an abandoned storefront lot.
3. Hide in the wooded area adjacent to the hospital.
4. Shoot Jasper with this unregistered gun when he comes out. *Thank you, Rex, for leaving this for me.*
5. Run back to my car.
6. Return to UBB.
7. ???

And then what? *The police would come knocking at my door, throw cuffs on me, read me my Miranda rights, and eventually, place me in a cell where I will rot out the rest of my days. All of this because of Jasper Merwood.*

C'mon, Cheryl, patience, think straight. No rash behavior. You got this. You've always been good at biding your time.

CHAPTER 24

Summer 2003

Paige Dawson, Paige Dawson, Paige Dawson! I am sick and tired of hearing about Paige Dawson! She is nothing more than a husband-stealing slut!

She lives in the lap of luxury, with all of Edward Merwood's money, and meanwhile, she's out fooling around with other people's men while ignoring her own son. She is disgusting. And don't get me started on her movies. They are trash! I have no idea what anybody sees in her. But now, she has an Oscar and a big head. There is no reason she should have that life. She doesn't deserve it with what she tried to do to my life!

When I heard she would be just a couple of hours away for the premiere of her new movie, I decided it was time to reignite our friendship…so to speak.

*****

"Hello?"

"Paige? Is that you?" I say with a hint of excitement.

"Yes. Who is this?"

"Paige, it's me, Cheryl Maxwell. Philip gave me this number. Do you remember me?"

"Cheryl! Sweetie, of course, I remember you. What a surprise! How are you doing?"

"I am wonderful. I saw you would be in Cleveland for the premiere of your new movie. I am so excited to see it. And with you just a couple of hours away, I thought maybe I could drive out, and we could meet up for some drinks after the showing. I know a great place right down by the lake."

"That would be spectacular! Oh, but, darling, can we meet here in my hotel room? You know how it is when I go out: the fans, the cameras, the paparazzi. They won't leave me alone. It's tough being famous, but I guess you know a little about that, right, with your Olympic fame?"

"The hotel room will be perfect." I tried to hold back the sarcasm. *How dare you compare your accomplishments to mine.*

"This is just so fabulous! So you will be attending the premiere?"

"Oh, yes, I wouldn't miss it, Paige."

"It is going to be a long night. After the showing, I have a number of commitments with the local media. Cleveland has been so wonderful throughout the filming, and they are superexcited we decided to do the premiere here. Then, we have a big after-party—"

"That does sound like a lot. So if meeting up tonight doesn't work, we can do it another time." *Don't you dare ruin this for me, Paige.*

Paige insisted, "No, no, no, Cheryl, I am thrilled to reconnect. I had so much fun with all of you at Philip's wedding! Anyway, I am going to need to wind down after this exciting day."

You mean you had fun with my husband, don't you?

"Okay, I can't wait to see you. Just tell me when and where."

"I'm in a private suite at the Drury on the sixth floor. Come on up around 10:00 PM. I can't wait to catch up with you, my darling. Will your beautiful daughter...Alicia...be joining us?"

"My daughter is Patricia. No, Paige, unfortunately, Trish is busy tonight. It will just be the two of us. See you later." I hung up and began preparing for my trip.

*****

I arrived at the agreed-upon time, and Paige greeted me with a smile and a hug as if we were truly old friends. Taking my hand, she led me into the sitting room.

"This is so much fun. It reminds me of simpler times, just hanging with friends. I even ordered us some room service. Tina Marie usually takes care of these things for me, but I let her stay at the social gatherings on my behalf so you and I could visit. Please sit down. We have so much to catch up on!"

I perched myself on the edge of the overstuffed couch and leaned toward the coffee table to pick up a couple of large bread cubes and dunk them in the spinach dip.

"Must be nice living in style," I stated as I popped the second cube into my mouth, taking in the massiveness and grandeur of the room.

"It has been a good life," Paige agreed. She handed me a bottle of Perrier, and we gestured a ceremonial toast to each other. Paige took a sip of water, but I asked if there was any bourbon.

"Bourbon? I would have figured you for only a Maxwell-made wine kind of girl." Paige winked at me as she headed to the decanters on the liquor cabinet across the room.

While Paige's back was turned, I took the opportunity to empty a vial of tranquilizer into her water.

Oh, Snow, even though more than a decade has passed, I still miss you.

"So I would ask you what you've been up to lately," I called out as I nonchalantly sat back into the cushions. "But it would be hard to not already be aware. I was glad you won the Oscar for *False Temptations*. I agreed with the Academy that you were spectacular in that film." *Yeah, right!*

"Oh, sweetie, thank you so much. It was quite an honor to get another award."

Paige set my drink beside the bread plate and returned to the chair opposite of me. She picked up her water and took another sip.

"I just wish Edward would have joined me. He has never been a fan of these ceremonies." She laughed meekly. "To be honest, I have never been his priority. No, his priority is making millions on developing properties and not on 'wasting' his time in the make-believe world of Hollywood. My assistant suggested I take Jasper, but, Cheryl, don't you agree this Hollywood scene isn't appropriate for a young boy?" Paige's voice trailed off slightly as she thought of her son.

"I totally understand that as a mother, you have to make difficult decisions that in the end are the most beneficial for your child." I chose my words carefully as I watched Paige drink more of the tainted water. "We all have to make choices, Paige."

"So tell me, Cheryl, how did you like the movie? I thought maybe I would see you there or even at the after-party," Paige asked.

"The movie? Paige, I didn't go to the movie. That's not why I am here."

Paige looked puzzled as she watched me slowly grab more bread and dip.

"Wait, then, why are you here?"

I leaned forward, resting my elbows on my knees, staring intently at Paige, and with sadistic pleasure, I whispered, "Oh, Paige, do you really think I don't know? You tried to ruin my life, and now, I'm ending yours."

"Cheryl…wait…what are you saying?" Paige slurred as she suddenly fell back in the chair. "I don't feel well. I think I need to lie down. Can you please get my phone so I can call my assistant?"

With her finger pointing in the direction of her purse, Paige went limp. Thankfully, I caught the bottle of water before it spilled on Paige's lap and onto the chair.

Whew. That was close. I can't take the risk of leaving evidence behind.

As requested, I did go to Paige's purse to retrieve her phone. But instead of calling her assistant, I erased my phone number from the call log, cleaned my fingerprints off, and dropped the phone back where I got it.

And would you look at that, right there in Paige's purse—a bottle of prescription sleeping pills. How fortunate for me. I brought my own unlabeled bottle as a decoy, but now, I won't need it. Finding an empty bottle of pills beside a spoiled actress, who would think anything but an overdose?

I dumped most of her pills into my own purse, staged the nearly empty pill bottle beside the untouched glass of bourbon, grabbed both bottles of water, and let myself out of the hotel suite, careful not to leave fingerprints on the door handle.

*****

The death of Paige Dawson was national news. Everyone who had ever worked with her was grabbing airtime to express their shock. "Paige had it all. I would never have suspected she was depressed," was the repeated mantra.

Not much was heard from her wealthy husband though. Edward Merwood and their already-sheltered son were kept out of the media's range. After a few days, the story of Paige's death went quiet.

CHAPTER 25

Present Time

Cheryl's memories were interrupted by the raindrop notification sound of her phone indicating a new text message.

Jasper. What already, Jasper? Can't you let an old lady reminisce in peace?

The message let Cheryl know that Tricia would be discharged from the hospital in a couple of hours, and then, he and Tricia needed to talk to her.

Okay, Jasper, we will talk. You can vent and put me in my place. I will let you have your day. I will wait for mine.

Cheryl scooped the gun off the desk and thought again about how reckless she had almost been. She started toward the staircase to return the gun to the bedroom. As she did, she made note of Trish's and Sterling's gifts arranged orderly underneath the tree. The vision reminded her of all the good times. The Maxwells had been so happy, or at least, they should have been. Trish had been challenging, but then again, what girl trying to find their way into adulthood isn't? How had Jasper Merwood gotten in and messed everything up? And why? She thought about that Thanksgiving six years earlier.

CHAPTER 26

November 2012

Tricia and Sterling arrived home at Unbreakable Bonds for Thanksgiving break late that Tuesday night. They were both exhausted from the long drive and headed right to bed. The next morning, I prepared some bacon, eggs, and toast and was sitting at the breakfast table when Tricia came downstairs.

"Hi, sweetie, welcome home. How did you sleep?"

"Okay, I guess," Trish mumbled, filling her plate to the brim. "I'm starving."

"You are welcome," I stated sarcastically, which was met with a roll of Trish's eyes. "So how are things at school?"

"Okay. I guess we'll know next week after finals." There was a pause in the conversation as Trish left it at that.

"Have you been studying?"

"No, Mom. I haven't studied at all!" Trish responded with much irritation.

"What's wrong with you?"

"Nothing. Can't I just eat in peace without getting the third degree?"

"Somebody woke up on the wrong side of the bed. Aren't you even going to ask me how things are here?"

Trish remained silent.

At that moment, Sterling came through the front door and made his way back to the kitchen.

"Oh man! Something smells amazing!"

"There's my Sterling! Are you hungry? Can I put a plate together for you?"

"I feel like I can eat a horse! Whoops, sorry, Mom." He laughed, realizing the slip with that phrasing. "Absolutely. Oh, scrambled eggs, yes, are they your three-cheese specialty?"

"They sure are."

"Thanks, Mom. I love you. It sure is nice to be home! How have things been here at good ole UBB?"

I gave Trish a sideways glance. *At least, someone cares about me.* Another eye roll was all I got in return.

"Things have been mostly good, Sterling. Thanks for asking. We are having a problem with some fencing out along the road that I hope you can help me with."

"Sure thing, Mom, I will check it out later this morning. I am going to take this plate with me down to the guesthouse. I want to get unpacked and settled in for the week. Thanks again. Hey, Trish, did you tell Mom about your new beau?" He laughed as he went out the back door and headed down the path to the guesthouse.

"You have a boyfriend?" I asked.

"Maybe" was Trish's evasive response.

"Are you going to tell me his name?"

"Well, since you probably won't leave me alone about it, his name is Jasper Merwood."

"Jasper Merwood? You have got to be kidding me! No! I will not have it."

"What are you talking about? Do you know him?" Trish responded, confused by my emphatic response.

I calmed just a notch, though it was hard with the bombshell I had just heard. "I know the family—"

Trish cut me off and increased her volume. "Mom, most people have heard of the Merwood family."

"Don't you remember? Phillip Dawson, our accountant, is the brother of Paige Dawson who was married to Edward Merwood. He wanted to take this farm from us. King Merwood knew we were struggling, and he tried lowballing me. I told Phillip to let them know we weren't for sale, and we never would be!" *Just the sound of that name irked me!*

"What does that have to do with Jasper?"

"Everything," I answered. "I bet you Edward told Jasper to seek you out. He doesn't like you for you, Trish. They are still just trying to get to this land."

"You have got to be freaking kidding me!" Throwing her fork down hard on her plate, Trish continued, "Why can't you ever just be happy for me, Mom? Why does it always have to be about this farm?"

"Trish, you are not to date Jasper Merwood! Do you hear me! I forbid it!"

"Just try to stop me, Mom!" Trish yelled as she stormed upstairs. Moments later, she had a bag packed and was headed out the front door. "I am leaving. Happy Thanksgiving, Mom. This sure has been fun."

"Where are you going, Trish? Let's talk about this."

"I'll find somewhere to enjoy the holiday. There is nothing for us to talk about. Oh, and I'm sure Sterling will be happy to stay here with you, so tell him he can find his own way back to school."

CHAPTER 27

Present Time

Cheryl entered her bedroom and placed the gun safely back in her nightstand. She had some time yet before Jasper and Trish would arrive, so she settled on the bed and continued to reminisce.

At first, she had been frustrated that Jasper and Trish were an item, but then as the relationship grew, she saw what was in front of her. The Maxwell fortune was nice. The Merwood fortune was in a whole other universe.

CHAPTER 28

September 2018

Edward had remarried, and his new wife was a disaster. All she did was spend the Merwood fortune.

I say "spend," but what I should say is "gives away."

Trish invited Sterling and me to Atlanta for yet another extravagant gala for charity hosted and funded by the Merwoods. The only worthwhile thing to come from Trish's marriage to the loathsome Jasper Merwood was access to the considerable estate, and at this rate, this new bimbo will blow through the whole thing by Christmas!

Sterling and I arrived in Atlanta in the early afternoon of Monday, September 3, and of course, we were picked up by a stretch limo that would have held a wedding party of twenty—comfortably.

Edward flaunting his wealth, he knows no other way.

As our ride to the estate began, my mind returned to the interactions I had had with Edward in the lean years of Unbreakable Bonds. Those were very unpleasant. I was at wit's end. Roger was ill, Trish and Sterling were away at school, and revenue was down. And this greedy billionaire was hounding me to sell the farm with lowball offers of no better than fifty cents on the dollar. The stress

I was under was unbearable at times, and it took quite the toll on my health. These memories were front and center in my mind as we arrived at the estate.

While I was obviously aware of the Merwood wealth, I was not at all prepared for how it would smack me in the face: the opulence, the outrageousness. There was crystal and granite everywhere. Beautiful hardwood furniture of ebony and mahogany lined the walls. Intricately carved ceilings towered above natural stone flooring. Rare and valuable artwork could be found both on the walls and resting on various furnishings, most lit under gold-trimmed fixtures. It was all so ostentatious. It made me sick. I hated the pretentiousness, arrogance, and confidence of this man.

Tricia met us in the great room, yes, the great room, and we had a warm embrace.

Soon, Tricia, this will all be yours…ours…very soon.

After settling into our luxurious bedrooms and spending some time relaxing by the large in-ground pool, we got dressed, and all of us went out on the town. What a rough night. I put on a happy face and covered up my downright disgust for Edward and his new Barbie. Oh, Lord, she acts like such a child. She doesn't take anything seriously, and if I had to hear that annoying, high-pitch squeal of a laugh one more time, I swear I would have taken the toxic dose of the sedative I brought with me on this trip myself.

Thankfully, the kids did most of the talking, reliving the various exploits and experiences they shared at the university. It was nice to see Sterling and Trish together, laughing and having a good time. It was also nice at the end of the evening to return to the Merwood estate and bury myself in that comfortable bed.

On Tuesday, I was able to rest and relax and for the most part steer clear of any awkward social situations with Edward and Emma. At the evening meal, Edward apologized for having to work the next day and outlined his full schedule of meeting with potential business partners. I paid rapt attention.

*****

The next morning, Tricia asked me to join her that evening at a new seafood restaurant in town. I begged off, telling her that I had planned an evening of pampering and shopping, and I was looking forward to it. I WAS looking forward to my evening, but it had nothing to do with shopping.

I sat alone at the Georgian Club that evening. I was in disguise, wearing a long black wig and tons of makeup. I watched Edward in all his glory, entertaining his foreign guests. That was fine. I think it was only right that he should enjoy his last meal.

Eventually, Edward and the Qataris finished their business. As Edward handled payment of his check, I made my way to the bar, striking up a quick conversation with Benjamin, the bartender.

"Hi there, miss, can I get you something to drink?" Benjamin offered.

"Please call me Jan. Just a water for me, but please make a mint julep for Edward," I responded in a voice that was a half octave deeper than my usual tone.

"Oh, do you have business with Mr. Merwood?" Benjamin inquired.

"I sure hope so… What was your name again?"

"Benjamin. My friends call me Benny," he responded.

"Benny it is then."

"My goodness, Jan, I am not usually this forward, but you smell amazing. What is that scent you are wearing?" Benny whispered as he leaned forward and handed me my water. He placed Edward's drink on the bar.

"Why, thank you, Benny. It's a personal blend of exotic oils. You like?"

"I definitely like," Benny said with a flirtatious smile.

"Benny, can I have a straw for my water?" I inquired. And as he turned to retrieve one, I quickly altered Edward's drink.

"Here you are, Jan, one straw."

"Benny, can you be a dear and get Edward's attention for me? Please let him know I just need a couple of minutes of his time. It will be worth his effort, I promise." I winked, picked up my water, and headed toward the entranceway. "I will be right back. Thanks, hon."

"It will be my pleasure. I look forward to the beautiful scent of Jan returning to my bar." Benny winked.

*****

I drove to a nearby fast food restaurant and dropped the wig in a dumpster. Inside, I went to the restroom and changed into a beautiful new dress and shoes that I had purchased earlier that evening. Then, I returned to the car and waited. Had it worked? If so, I anticipated I would receive a phone call. The wait seemed interminable, but finally, my phone buzzed. It was a text from Jasper with the wonderful news that Edward had passed. I had worked so hard to pull this off, and it felt good to meet such success. And to know that it would never lead back to me. Now, I had to rush to the hospital and present a front of sorrow and dismay that would totally belie my feelings of great joy and accomplishment.

*****

I was still on a high as we left the funeral and headed back to the reception at the Merwood Estate, but I also knew I still had work to do. As it had on many occasions today, my hands instinctively went to the pocket of the dark fashionable jacket I wore to the funeral and was once again comforted to feel the remaining vial of poison. I had purchased the jacket and the long black dress I wore beneath it on Wednesday evening before heading to the Georgian Club. I laughed quietly to myself as I considered the highly uncommon occurrence of purchasing funeral wear in advance of the sudden death of a heretofore healthy person.

Emma is really putting on quite a show. It started at the hospital, with all the tears and shrieks and the near fainting at the sight of Edward's lifeless body. *Oh, c'mon, gold digger, nobody is buying this act. I mean, cry me a river. You didn't love Edward, you loved his money, and now, it is all yours. Ha-ha, for a few more minutes anyway, I guess.*

Now, here we are back at the estate, and she is stepping it up a notch. I overheard her tell the butler that she was going to take a prescription sedative and rest upstairs for a while and did not want the others to know.

Probably so she can take a break from all this acting. That show has got to be tiring.

Of course, this couldn't possibly have set up any better for me.

Shortly before the meal, the minister offered apologies. He had another funeral to preside over and had to be on his way. He hoped to have the opportunity to give final condolences to Emma. I was fortunate enough to be nearby as he approached Emma's mother, Ronita. Ronita was not sure where Emma was and said she would go in search of her. I offered to help. I told Ronita to check the first floor, and I would look upstairs.

This was it. I would not have a better opportunity.

I emptied the vial in my drink as I reached the top of the stairs. As I started down the hall toward the master bedroom, I was startled by Emma calling my name as I passed the study.

"Cheryl? Is everything okay?"

"Oh, Emma, you scared me. I was just coming to find you. I thought you might be resting."

"I really do need some rest, and that was the plan, but my mind is still racing a million miles per hour. I have so many things that I need to get done, and it overwhelms me to think about them, and I want to talk to Edward, and that reminds me that he is dead, and then I crash again as the sadness floods back..." Her voice broke at that point. *Oh, she really is good! A better actress than Edward's first wife, the whore.*

"Oh, I can't even imagine, dear," I said comfortingly. *Ha-ha, I guess I have some acting skills too.* "Can I help you with something?" I said, offering her the drink. She declined. *Darn it.*

"Thank you, Cheryl. I was just looking for the check I wrote for the caterers, and I wanted to give something to Pastor William for the church before he goes."

Of course, she does. She just gives it all away. Well, I will be putting a stop to that.

"Here, I will help you look." As I did a cursory search of the large mahogany desk, Emma stepped out to the balcony and rested her hands on the far rail.

"Emma, are you okay?" I asked as I came out to meet her.

"Sorry, yes, I think I just need some fresh air to clear my head," Emma said as she peered down at the rock garden below her. "It is a pretty day out here, everything else withstanding."

"Yes, it is beautiful," I responded. "Here, have a drink. This should help," I said, once again offering her the tainted whiskey.

"No, thank you, Cheryl, I took some Valium a few minutes ago and don't believe I should mix alcohol with that."

Unbelievable!

"Oh, Cheryl, what am I going to do? I don't know how to live without Edward."

Oh god, she is starting up again.

"Well, you have all that money, and this house, and like a bazillion properties," I blurted out of frustration.

She looked up at me in shock. "I don't care about any of that! I would give it all up for just one more day with Edward." She then threw herself up against the balcony railing, using it to steady herself.

I thought I was going to barf, but suddenly, plan B was right in front of me. I quickly grabbed Emma around the waist and hoisted her in one swift move, propelling her over the edge. She let out one final scream as she plunged to her death.

At that very moment as Emma toppled over the railing, I heard a gasp from the entryway of the study. I turned and was rocked by the sight of Sterling, standing there, mouth agape. I recovered from my surprise almost instantly and screamed, "Emma, No! No, Emma! Oh my god! No!" I watched as Sterling, with the strangest of looks on his face, turned and raced back down the stairs. I paused momentarily, knew I would need to talk to Sterling about this later, and then offered myself a congratulatory pat on the back.

Boy, did that feel good. Now everyone just needs to buy the notion that Emma was so distraught that she did herself in.

I ran down the stairs, tears flowing freely.

"No, Emma, Why? No!" *Ha-ha, Emma, I will show you how this grief acting is really done.*

*****

Later that evening, Sterling and I found some quiet time. Just as I had done with the police a couple of hours earlier, I explained how I tried to calm Emma down.

"She had so much to live for, but she wouldn't hear it. Her mind was made up. As she fell, I tried to grab her, catching her around the waist, but I just didn't have the strength to stop the fall."

I am not convinced that Sterling believed me, but I do know that Sterling is a good boy who will never disappoint his mother.

*****

After a few more days in Atlanta consoling Jasper, Sterling and I left Merwood estate behind and returned to Westfield, New York, and to the affairs of UBB.

CHAPTER 29

December 18, 2018

I was in a light mood as I headed to the large desk that sat adjacent to the sparsely stocked bar in the den. I even laughed as I stepped on the squeaky floorboard that lay in front of the rarely utilized fireplace. That floorboard had been loose since before I even came to this place. I can't remember how many times I asked Rex to fix it. Usually hearing the loose board would cause me a quick jolt of frustration or anger, but not today. Today, I laughed.

I was following the "suspicious" death of Edward Merwood very closely, and everything I had read online earlier this morning suggested the case was stagnate and growing cold. The police knew the death was caused by an overdose of barbiturates or maybe the combination of barbiturates and alcohol; they just could not determine a source of the drugs. Had Edward been taking something for insomnia or anxiety or depression? There was no indication that he had been. Had his business meeting with the Qataris gone sour? Everyone involved said the dinner had been very positive, and the project was moving forward. And who was the young lady who wanted to talk to Edward but left before she got the opportunity?

Ahhh, Benny remembered me.

The daughter of a jilted business partner? An unhappy mistress that was tired of hiding in the shadows? An expected attendee of the charity gala the next day? Did Emma set this up and then commit suicide? Emma was a headline in her own right. Why had she jumped to her death the day of Edward's funeral? *If only they knew, but they never will.*

The investigation was going nowhere. And so I was happy, and the floorboard squeaked, and I laughed…

I was in the den to check the latest postings from a national news website when my accountant, Phillip Dawson, called and said he was on his way over. He needed acquisition papers for the hay baler we had purchased just three years prior. That piece of equipment had not been performing well this fall, and Phillip wanted to alter the depreciation schedule for it, as well as a horse trailer which had seen better days. I had better things to think about, but Phillip insisted we take care of this right away.

Phillip arrived within a few minutes. He entered the den and stepped on the same loose board as I had. Phillip also laughed.

"You still have the secret compartment, I hear."

"Hi, Phil. The what?" I questioned.

"The compartment where Rex hid all his important…uhh… things."

"Are you serious? That's why that board is loose?"

"I can't believe you were unaware of it." Phillip laughed and continued, "Yeah, when Rex and Roger were young, that's where they kept all their favorite magazines, if you know what I mean. And they always had a nice stash of marijuana."

"Boys." I scoffed.

"He also kept his first gun down there as well. It was a 1935 Smith & Wesson .357 revolver, a secret gift from his grandfather. I wonder what ever happened to that old gun? Oh, and he always stashed a little cash down there too, just in case the police showed up, and he and Roger had to make a run for it." Phillip, still laughing, added, "You never know, you should take a look. You may be rich.

And, tell you what, give me 10 percent, and we won't even throw it on this year's tax return."

"Ha-ha. Thanks, Phillip, I will have to check that out. And how about 8 percent? Final offer!"

We both laughed.

I was extremely curious about what lay beneath that floorboard, and the next half hour with Phillip felt eternal. By the end, I was practically pushing him out the door. After he left, I waited a few moments and then headed to the garage to gather a couple of tools.

I headed back to the den, and using the chisel and mallet, I raised the pesky board as well as the two boards on either side. Sure enough, I spotted a large metal box, about two feet long, one foot wide and another foot deep. I went to open the box, but it was locked. I cursed under my breath and then went to the desk, the desk that old Mr. Maxwell had built when he started Unbreakable Bonds. Even though Rex had added on to the back of the house for a more appropriately located office, he never wanted to move his father's desk. I guess neither did I after all these years. I knew the long drawer across the front center of the desk had several keys for which I was not sure the purpose. I tried one and then another without any luck. The third key gave the satisfying clicking sound as it entered and opened the lock. I opened the lid.

The first thing that caught my eye was the old pistol that Phillip had described. I pulled it out for a moment, admiring it, and then set it aside.

The only other item in the box was a large manila envelope, bulging, filled with something. Could this be the stash of cash? As I pulled it out, I was hit with the very faint smell of something? Perfume?

I flipped the envelope over, loosened the clasp, and peered inside. My stomach sank immediately. Instead of a wad of cash, I pulled out a stack of letters. I read the return addressee: Paige Dawson.

Love letters!

How romantic of you to save these, Rex.

I debated whether to read them or toss them in the fireplace. I had nothing else to do, so I poured myself a glass of wine and settled in for some entertaining reading.

*****

> October 15, 1990: My Dearest Rex, words cannot describe how I am feeling right now. My time with you at UBB was the most alive I have felt in I don't know how long. The way you and I connected was amazing. I keep thinking about our walks and time spent in the winery showroom, talking about everything under the sun. I miss you so much already, and it's only been a few days since my brother's wedding. I wish I could rewind time...

I bet you really wish that now. I tossed that letter aside and opened another from further in the stack.

> September 15, 1991: Thank you for the beautiful letter, my love... I miss you... I can't wait to be together again... I have cleared my schedule to be able to join you at the Napa Valley Harvest Festival next week... I cannot wait to be in your arms again

How could you, Rex? I was six months pregnant with our daughter, and you were planning escapades with your tramp!
This time, I grabbed a letter from nearer to the bottom.

> January 20, 1992: Rex, darling, I have some wonderful news! I am sorry you have to hear this in a letter, but I don't dare take the chance of calling you in case Cheryl is around... I am

**pregnant... We have so much to talk about... I
want us to be a family...**

I began to hyperventilate to the point that I nearly passed out.
I took a minute to try to compose myself but was finding that to be
impossible. I dropped the letter and slid off the chair and onto the
floor.

What? Rex is the father of...of...Jasper?

I don't know how long I stayed there on my knees, in pure
shock. I couldn't bear reading any more of those deceitful letters, so
I stuffed them back in the manila envelope and tossed it in the desk
drawer. I knew I had to tell Tricia. I would have to get Jasper and
Tricia apart.

*****

"Hi, Trish, it's your mother."

"Yes, Mom, I know. What's wrong? Why are you calling so late?"

"Trish, there's something very important happening, and I need
to you to come home immediately...and alone."

"What's this about? You're scaring me. Are you okay? Is Sterling
okay?"

"We're both fine. I can't get into this over the phone, but please
just get here as quickly as you can. I cannot overemphasize how much
I need you here."

"Okay." Tricia was worried. She had never heard her mother
like this before. "Why can't Jasper come? Whatever this is, maybe he
could help."

"Trish! Please just do as I ask and come alone. Can you be here
tomorrow?"

Tricia knew by the tone in her mother's voice she wasn't getting
any information over the phone, and she was not to bring Jasper.

"Yes, Mom, I'll leave first thing in the morning."

"I love you, Tricia. I really do love you."

CHAPTER 30

Present Time

Before Cheryl got off the bed, she texted Jasper and apologized for the past week. She wrote, "I am sure by now you are aware of the horrific news that I became aware of just last week. I hope you can imagine the trauma I have been feeling. I handled it so very poorly, and I understand completely your anger with me. I just hope you can forgive me. I look forward to our discussions this afternoon."

Yuck! That was excruciating to write. She headed downstairs as the memory of that heartbreaking conversation with Tricia just a few days ago came flooding back.

CHAPTER 31

December 19, 2018, 9:00 AM

"Mom, I'm here!" Tricia called out as soon as she opened the front door. She tossed her bags at the base of the staircase and headed for the kitchen. There she found me, dressed in my usual jeans and tucked-in flannel shirt, hair in a ponytail.

"Trish, oh my Trish," I practically whispered as I rose up to give my daughter a warm embrace.

"Mom, Mom, you're scaring me. You got me here. Now, tell me what is going on."

I could tell my greeting worried her, so I figured I might as well just get to it.

"Sit down. I need to tell you something."

*****

I spent the next hour giving what seemed like a history lesson. I regurgitated how much I loved UBB from the moment I took my first riding lesson with Sandy. I replayed the history of the exciting Olympic times, the courtship between her father and me, and our friendship with the Shapiros and how we came to know Paige Dawson, and by default, Edward Merwood. I reminded her of how after Snow and her dad died, I was struggling with the business aspects of UBB, and Edward tried to buy me out. Tricia had heard all this at various times throughout her life, and while at first, she just let me talk, I could feel her impatience growing.

Before I could get to the point, Tricia interjected, "Mom, you're not telling me anything I don't already know. What I need you to tell me is why I am here now."

I had spent most of last evening and this morning planning this conversation and what would follow. I had to be very careful.

"You're right. Here goes." I took a deep breath and prepared for an extreme reaction from Trish to this news. Would she faint? Would she get angry and storm out to find Sterling, or worse yet, call Jasper? I refilled our coffee mugs and added three Xanax tablets to Tricia's. I hated to do this, but I had to retain control of the situation.

"Trish. I need to talk to you about Jasper. Are you happy?"

"What kind of question is that?" Trish took a long swig of her tainted coffee as she gave me a disgusted look.

I hate that look. She was always so quick to judge me.

I tried to stay calm and let the sedatives take effect. "I just mean…is this marriage everything you want it to be? I know Jasper is preoccupied with the death of his father and stepmother. I hear the news. There is still an investigation into Edward's death. And with Jasper trying to run the company and deal with all of this, you've said he is drinking a lot, and you don't spend much time together."

"Mom, thanks for your concern, but my marriage is really none of your business. You've never really approved of my relationship with a Merwood. For some reason, you think they were out to get you. As if the Unbreakable Bonds was of any importance to the billionaire Edward Merwood. Really, Mom, you brought me all the way out here just to talk about Jasper?"

"Please calm down, Trish—" I was interrupted by another outburst from Trish.

"You always do this. You make everything about you, and you've never wanted me to be happy!" Even though she was mad, I could tell the pills were working.

I just sat there for a moment as Trish raised the mug to her lips…or tried to, I should say.

*****

"Sterling, I need you to come up to the house immediately. Something is wrong with Tricia." I hung up and carefully moved Trish to the sofa in the living room.

It only took a minute for Sterling to come bursting through the door.

"What's wrong with Trish?"

"She and I were talking about her current situation with Jasper. He is not good to her, Sterling. He stays out drinking all the time and comes home mean. She's at her wit's end and was very anxious. The next thing I knew, she passed out. We need to get her to a hospital. Sterling, listen to me carefully. Jasper cannot know about this."

Sterling and I carried Trish out to my car and headed for Westfield Memorial Hospital. Tricia never woke up, and thankfully, my friend, Dr. Richard Alexander, was on call. I had her admitted for her own safety to the psychiatric ward for observation. I explained she was under a lot of stress and may have purposely overdosed; she may become combative when she comes to. Richard agreed to keep her sedated until I could get more information.

I bought myself some time…but not much.

CHAPTER 32

December 20, 2018, 3:00 PM

"Cheryl, how are you doing?" Jasper asked. I was expecting to hear from him.

"Hi, Jasper, I am fine. What brings me the pleasure of this call?"

"Is Trish there, Cheryl? I really need to talk to her, and she has her phone off."

"Well, Jasper, do you blame her? You certainly haven't made things easy for her the past couple of months. We all feel terrible for you and everything you are dealing with, but you also need to remember that Tricia is on your team." I continued, "That said, she is not here."

"She's not there? Where is she?" Jasper's voice rose a bit.

I was in a tricky spot here, and I needed to walk a tight rope with this conversation. I had to keep him in New York another day. I certainly didn't want him coming out to the farm.

"She left this morning, Jasper. We had a fight, and I finally convinced her that she should go home, and that you two needed to work this out one way or another. So I believe she is coming home, but I am not sure when you should expect her. I believe Tricia's exact words were 'I think I will take my time. I am definitely not in a hurry to get back.'" *That should do it.*

"Okay, thanks, Cheryl. I am going to make things right."

Sure you will, Jasper. Not if I make things right first, though.

CHAPTER 33

Present Time

Cheryl went to the kitchen and started boiling some water. It had been a long day for all of them. The evening conversation would surely be difficult whether Jasper accepted her apology or not. She figured a warm family meal couldn't hurt. She pulled a couple of chicken breasts from the freezer and threw them in the microwave to thaw. Then, she grabbed a box of fettucine noodles and a jar of Alfredo sauce from the pantry.

Two days ago, I never would have thought I would be cooking Jasper Merwood a meal this evening.

CHAPTER 34

December 21, 2018, 6:00 PM

Jasper Merwood stood among the hordes on the subway platform in the early evening hours of this the last Friday before Christmas. The crowd was quite merry. And in the spirit of the season, they were uncharacteristically patient, polite, and even friendly. They were responding positively to the ringing bells at the Salvation Army buckets and generously giving to the poor, homeless souls bundled up within the subway halls and staircases. Many carried packages in various stages of wrap, some the spoils of office-party grab bags, and others set to be gifted at romantic dinners or under beautifully decorated trees. They were singing along with Bing Crosby to the familiar lyrics of "White Christmas" as it played over the subway speakers.

I couldn't believe my luck.

Go ahead, Jasper, step a little closer to the edge of that platform.

I could hear the faint roar of the Queens express and immediately decided to make my move. I deftly made my way through the crowd until I was directly behind Jasper. Even if he turned around now, he would not recognize me with this gaudy winter getup complete with New York Jets tassel cap, scarf, and oversize sunglasses.

It's not your fault, Jasper. Not all of it. But you will pay the price.

I ducked my shoulder and raised it into Jasper's back, sending him over the edge.

Goodbye, Jasper. I will comfort Tricia for you.

I quickly blended into the crowd. At first, I heard the screams, then came the cheering.

Cheering? These fools are cheering because a man just got smashed by an oncoming train? Unbelievable! You have more lives than a cat, you bastard!

As I was pretending to be lost in a text conversation on my phone, I saw Jasper looking around at all the passengers surrounding him on the platform.

He began to regain his nerves and asked no one in particular, "Did you see what happened? Was I pushed?"

Yeah, Jasper, I saw it. I pushed you. You should be a pancake glued to the front of that train. Instead, Mr. Hero saved your life. Not a big deal. This wasn't the plan anyway. I'm not finished here.

I tapped my bag with the vial of sodium pentobarbital concealed inside. I will finish this tonight and still be home to celebrate Trish's birthday in the morning. Once out of the subway, I hailed for my hired driver.

"Bruno, we're headed back to the Uptown Luxury Suites," I instructed as I settled into the back seat of the BMW.

*****

Since the attempt on Jasper's life in the subway was thwarted, *I just have to stick with the original plan of poisoning him. Let's run through that plan one more time.*

First, I will make a surprise entrance under the guise of needing to share some very important information with him about Tricia. I know he's been trying to contact her unsuccessfully since I have her phone, so I am sure he will invite me in with open arms.

He'll pour us a drink, and we'll sit down for a chat. After I know he has ingested the poison, I'll tell him about the affair between his mother and Tricia's father. He will be beside himself with grief. I will be giddy but not outwardly so.

As he begins to fade, I will tell him how I killed his mother, father, and stepmother. He will struggle to comprehend what I am telling him. He won't understand my need to kill his family. It will be torture. It will be so much fun.

Not that I have anything against Jasper directly. I've never really taken to him, but then again, I've never really tried too hard either. In all seriousness, he is a Maxwell, and that fact puts the farm in danger. Would he try to take it from me? Who is to say? More importantly, with all the Merwoods dead and Jasper and Tricia's marriage technically legal, Tricia and I will inherit billions!

"Bruno, I'll be back in about thirty minutes."

Jasper? What is he doing back out here?

I watched as Jasper reemerged through the front door of the apartment building and jumped into a waiting cab.

"Bruno, follow that cab!"

*****

Interesting choice, Jasper, so lo mein for your last meal, is it?

This would work as good as any place. I hopped out of the car and entered the Dim Sum Palace.

I weaved my way through the crowd toward the rear of the restaurant.

Ah, there you are! I'll be back for you, my friend.

I made a quick turn toward the ladies' room but stopped when I realized he was practically looking straight through me and was fixated on something…someone…else.

"Now, there's a sight for sore eyes. Hello, Mary," Jasper said as he stood and embraced a woman.

Who is that? I know that face. Mary? Mary…Mary Sintag! That's it. She's Tricia's friend from college. But why is she meeting Jasper here tonight?

I continued to the ladies' room to gather my thoughts. Mary Sintag, the cop-turned-PI that has been all over the news lately is meeting Jasper. He's up to something, and I need to stop him now.

I returned to the front of the restaurant and asked to be seated at a small table in the rear. The table I selected strategically allowed me to place my back to Jasper and Mary, and I was privy to their conversation. I ordered a glass of wine and a small plate of dumplings and began to sleuth.

"Clearly, she didn't come straight home," Mary was saying.

Nice private eye observation there. Hope you are paying her good, Jasper.

Jasper was obviously concerned, and toward the end of the conversation, I heard Mary say, "We will go to the farm tomorrow."

You have got to be kidding me! What the heck! This was not what I wanted to hear, but at least, I was armed with this information, and now, I could formulate a plan to mitigate the danger.

A few minutes later, Jasper and Mary made their way out of the Dim Sum Palace, and I began to act.

I called Sterling. "Sterling, listen, Jasper will be at the farm tomorrow. I will be back in Westfield very early in the morning, and I will get an Uber home. I am leaving Tricia's car at the train station. Sterling, our story is that Trish left the farm in her car on Thursday morning around eleven o'clock."

Jasper, you live to see another day.

CHAPTER 35

Present Time

Cheryl was setting the table for three, and then, she remembered Mary.

Would that nosy investigator be joining them this evening?

Jasper had not mentioned her, but Cheryl thought she better check. She sent him a text to confirm. After a few minutes, Cheryl checked her phone. Nothing yet from Jasper.

Might as well just assume Mary is coming. Swell.

She grabbed a bottle of wine from the built-in cabinet beneath the kitchen island and placed it in the center of the table and went for another place setting.

As she turned back to check the noodles, she thought back to the crazy day she had yesterday. Jasper and his investigator friend had shown up at her door at the farmhouse just mere hours after she had returned from New York City.

CHAPTER 36

December 22, 2018, 2:00 PM

I barely got any sleep, and when I did wake up, I had a text from Jasper. He and Mary would be here—in less than fifteen minutes. I barely had time to take a shower, throw on a robe, and wrap my hair in a towel when the security guard announced through the intercom that I had guests. *Uninvited guests.*

I angrily made my way downstairs and threw open the door as Jasper prepared to knock.

"Jasper, I don't know why you came all the way out here. I told you Tricia isn't here."

"Cheryl, you remember Mary Sintag, Tricia's friend from college. She's a private investigator now."

"I remember you, Mary. What possibly brings you to UBB today? Do you get called into these domestic squabble cases often?"

"Hello again, Cheryl. Jasper has good reason to feel this is much more serious than that. Trish hasn't made it home, and we can't reach her by phone. Can you tell us when the last time was you saw your daughter?"

"Jasper, this is crazy. Maybe if you spent a little less time at the office or in the bars, you wouldn't be in this predicament."

I invited them in for coffee.

Only because I had to.

I couldn't believe all the nosy questions Mary was asking. Even though Tricia held some grudge against me, I was a good mother and always did what was best for my daughter. How dare this woman come into my home and grill me like this!

The phone rang. It was Sterling.

"Good afternoon, Sterling."

"Mom, I'm glad you made it back safely. I just got back from seeing Trish. Is that Jasper's car?"

"Yes, I got back very early this morning. That is Jasper's car. He is here with Mary Sintag. They are looking for Trish. I told them she left here Thursday."

"I thought of what to say after you called last night. I can talk to Jasper to calm him down."

"Are you sure that's a good idea?"

"I got this, Mom. Jasper and Trish are going through a rough patch. Let me help."

"Okay."

"You know I won't reveal where Trish really is. Just let me calm him down until she is strong enough to talk to him. Send him down to the barn."

"Of course, I will send him down."

I sent Jasper to the barn to talk with Sterling, but that meant I was stuck alone with Mary.

Oh the joy!

"Mary, I really wish you wouldn't have come here. I just got back from a business trip that didn't go as planned, and I was hoping to get some rest."

I don't like how Mary is looking at me. Play it cool, Cheryl.

"Mary, I don't know what Tricia has told you, but let me share a few things with you. Trish was such a pleasant little girl. From an early age, she enjoyed being with me at the stables, brushing the horses, and cantering in the corrals. I had such high hopes for her as an equestrian…maybe even a second-generation Olympic gold med-alist. But by the time she was a teenager, we had grown distant. She was spending less and less time with me and more time alone in her room. I just passed it off as normal teenage-girl angst, always battling with her mother. Sometimes, she would run out of the house and spend the night with the Shapiros in the guesthouse. I guess she was making the point that she wanted to get away from me."

"So you and she would fight often?" Mary asked.

"No, I wouldn't say often, Mary. Probably relatively standard as far as these things go. As you know, she took up writing, and that preoccupied all her time. She would always be writing about what was happening at school and in the community. It seemed she was more interested in other people's lives than her own mother or this farm. But as long as I let her do what she wanted, we got along. When she didn't get her way, we fought."

"Tricia is a very talented writer, Cheryl. Have you read some of her work in the *New York Times*?"

"Of course, I have, Mary, she's my daughter. I was incredibly proud to see her story about Edward Merwood that ran on the front page for three straight days. I strutted around town showing every-body we knew."

"It didn't bother you that Tricia was giving such accolades to Edward Merwood? I heard you weren't his biggest fan."

"Mary, I didn't say I liked the subject. I said I was proud of my daughter."

"Sorry, Cheryl, I didn't mean to imply that you didn't show interest in Tricia's work. I just think you should understand that she loves writing like you love riding horses. You shouldn't hold it against her."

As if I need Mary to tell me anything about my daughter. I love Tricia and will do anything for her. Anything.

"I know, Mary. I'm sorry I snapped. I'm just tired from my trip and wasn't prepared for this surprise visit."

"Cheryl, can you tell me anything about the last time you saw Tricia? The tiniest of detail might be what we need to figure out where she is."

Why won't she just give this PI attitude a rest?

"Mary, like I told you earlier, Trish and I had an argument about her and Jasper's relationship. She said she was heading home but would take her time getting there. So while I don't know exactly where she is, I'm sure she is fine. I expect to hear from her any minute."

At that moment, Jasper returned from the barn with Sterling.

This is one of the few times I can say I am happy to see him.

"Well? Anything?" Jasper said without greeting.

"Nothing really," answered Mary.

"We need to file a missing-person report and get some help in this search."

"I am very worried about Tricia myself, Jasper. But I was just telling Mary a few moments ago that Trish does have a history of running off when she gets angry with me. Give me a little time to make some calls around town to see if I can learn anything before we involve the authorities."

Jasper reluctantly agreed. "Mary and I will go check into the Lake View Motel. It's probably the only place open during the off-season. You have one hour, and then, I am going to the police station."

"Jasper, if you would have given me more notice, you could have stayed here. Sorry, but I'm just not prepared to host the two of you. Nonetheless, there is no need to stay at such a seedy place. I will give my friends Harry and Susan Broadmoar a call. They own the Oak Barrel Bed and Breakfast in Fredonia, and they can put you and Mary up for the night."

"Thanks, Cheryl. Tell them we're on our way." Jasper gave Sterling a nod goodbye and headed toward the door.

As soon as the door closed behind them, I laid into Sterling.

"Really, Sterling? You agree that a missing-person report needs to be filed with the police? What were you thinking?"

"Sorry, Mom, but Jasper is really upset. I didn't tell him to do it, but I couldn't get him off this track. You saw him. He truly misses Tricia and wants to make things work. We have to tell him Tricia is okay. We have to help them repair this marriage."

"We have to do no such thing! Since when do you question my judgment? I know what is best for Tricia, and Jasper just isn't it anymore."

"But Jasper is insistent. If you don't give him information within the hour, he will go to the police. Then, how will it look when everyone finds out we've been lying? I hate seeing my friend suffering so much. And for what? Why are you putting him through this? Tricia was a shell of herself this morning. She is broken and scared about something, something deeper than Jasper acting like a jerk. What aren't you telling me?"

"Sterling, my dear, I have always protected you and Tricia. I am just doing what I think is best. Please trust me on this."

"I don't like this one bit."

"All right, Sterling, you win. I'll go check Tricia out of the hospital and tell Jasper to meet us back here later. But first, I need to call the Broadmoars. Promise me you won't talk to Jasper until after I talk to Trish."

"Okay, Mom, I promise."

Sterling headed back to the barn, and I dialed the Broadmoars.

"Hello, Susan, this is Cheryl Maxwell. How are you today? Good. Fine here, thank you. I hope you don't mind, but I am calling to ask a favor. My son-in-law and his friend unexpectedly came for a visit, and my guest rooms are being remodeled. I know you are closed for the season, but by any chance, do you have two rooms that you could host them for one night? Fabulous. I appreciate this very much. Jasper will be arriving shortly. Goodbye, and give my best to Harry please."

CHAPTER 37

December 22, 2018, 3:30 PM

I was just pulling into the hospital parking lot to visit Tricia for her birthday when I answered the call on the third ring.

"Hi, Jasper, are you situated over there at the Oak Barrel?"

Jasper ignored my question and the formalities. "Cheryl, any luck? What have you learned?"

Well, Jasper, for one thing, I have learned you are a real pain in the butt.

"I put feelers out all over town. I spoke to some friends as well as the local business owners who know Tricia. Everyone is aware that I have upset her again, and she took off. They know we are worried about her, and that you are in town looking for her.

"Jasper, I understand you are very concerned," I continued in a calmer, reassuring voice. "But Trish is okay. Once she finds out you are here, she will reach out. By this time tomorrow, you two will be together. I am sure of it. I mean, I'm her mother. Certainly, I would sense if something was wrong."

"Thanks, Cheryl. I hope you are right," was all Jasper said before clicking off.

Jasper, I'm always right.

*****

"Hello, birthday girl!" I said as I entered Trish's hospital room. I hated that she was in the mental ward, but I had no choice. If I handled this conversation correctly, I would be bringing Tricia home to deal with the Jasper situation together. If it went poorly, well, I'd resort to the backup plan.

"I'm surprised to see you here, M-o-t-h-e-r," Trish replied, accentuating the formal word. "Why am I here? What happened? Sterling came to see me earlier and said I had passed out."

"Yes, honey, we were talking at the kitchen table, and you dropped your coffee. I couldn't get you to respond to me. I was very concerned, so Sterling and I brought you here. Are you comfortable? Is Dr. Alexander taking good care of you?"

"If you call keeping me drugged and locked in my room comfortable, then yes, I'm as snug as a bug in a rug. But you didn't answer my question as to why I am here. What were we talking about just before I went out? I believe you were about to tell me why you called frantically for me to come see you, and then, all you wanted to do was talk about your life at UBB and how bad of a husband Jasper is."

I could tell this wasn't going well, but I just had to spit it out. I told her how I found the letters and that Jasper was most definitely her half brother.

Unfortunately, her reaction was worse than I expected. At first, she was in shock. Total silence filled the room for what felt like an eternity. Then, she started to cry as the reality of the situation sank in. I tried to calm her, to soothe her, to just be her mother. But no, typical Tricia, she started screaming at me and throwing accusations that somehow this was my fault. She created such a ruckus that the nurse came in and administered a sedative into her IV line, much to her objection.

Someday, Trish, you will understand.

CHAPTER 38

Present Time

The food was done and warming on the stove. Cheryl would have thrown in some broccoli, but Sterling always vetoed it. "Broccoli is for the horses," he would say. She went to the back door and stared down at the guesthouse. This was always a beautiful view, especially after a snowfall like last night. But not on this day. Crime-scene tape and flashing lights from the remaining police car stole the scene.

Why are the police still there?

CHAPTER 39

December 22, 2018, 5:00 PM

I returned from the hospital and sat down on the couch. Jasper and Mary were asking too many questions. I had to put a stop to that.

A few minutes later, Sterling came through the back door. "Mom? Trish? Are you guys here?"

"Hey, Sterling. In the living room."

Sterling came back. "Hi, Mom. I thought maybe Trish would have been with you."

"No, Sterling. She is not ready yet. I had to leave her there."

"But—" Sterling started.

I stopped him short. "Honey, I have had a long day. I haven't eaten since breakfast. Do you think we could have some dinner and talk about something else for a bit?"

"Sure, how was your trip?"

"Is salad okay?" I asked, pulling some fresh vegetables from the crisper. "It was a pretty boring conference to be honest, but I did get some information on a potential new bottle supplier," I lied and changed the subject. "How about this snowstorm we are expecting tonight? Any concerns down at the barn?"

"I fixed the issue with the ventilation of the space heater. Good thing too, otherwise the horses might have been in for a long winter's nap."

"Well, I am sure they appreciate that, sweetie. Hey, why don't you come over here and start chopping the lettuce."

We worked in silence for a while, finishing prepping dinner and setting the table. My mind was lost in my own thoughts when Sterling suddenly said, "Sure was nice to see Jasper today!"

"What did you two talk about?" I asked with a hint of uneasiness.

"Mom, he is a mess. He really misses Trish. He is so disappointed with how he has treated her and is ready to make it right."

"I don't know about that!" I snapped. "I can tell you Tricia does not want to see him."

"Mom, why do you say that? I was just with Trish this morning. I would say she is lost and confused, but she didn't say anything about leaving Jasper. She wants things back the way they were," Sterling said.

If only he knew.

"Sterling, Jasper and Tricia will never be back together. We cannot allow it."

Sterling was caught off guard by both my tone and the finality of my statement. "Mom, it is not our call! We need to tell Jasper where Trish is and let them work it out!"

"We will do no such thing, Sterling!" I shouted. "You will listen to your mother!"

"Mom, I love you, but this is wrong. Jasper deserves to know. He has been through so much, and this is killing him."

"Then, let him die! Jasper is not my concern. Tricia is. You are. We need to worry about us. I could care less about the Merwoods."

"What an awful thing to say, Mom. What has gotten into you? Jasper is our family. And, seriously, what did the Merwoods ever do to you? Mom, did you push Emma Merwood?"

Where did THAT come from?

"Sterling! We talked about that months ago. I tried to save that witch. How dare you accuse me! Just let it go. Do not disappoint me, Sterling!" I screamed.

154

"I am telling Jasper where Trish is! And I think maybe we need to talk about Emma again. You want me to drop it, but I know what I saw. I know my mother is not behaving like the person I have known and loved all my life! I don't know what has gotten into you." With that, Sterling stormed out and headed back down to the guesthouse.

My mind was racing. Not my Sterling, my ever-loyal son.

Are you going to betray me? Don't you see what needs to be done?

I needed to convince him because if he was not part of the solution, then he was part of the problem. With that thought, I choked back a tear.

I knew. I knew what had to be done. I went to the bedroom and grabbed a trusty vial of pentobarbital from my stash in the back of the closet. Again, I tried to choke back the emotion welling up inside me. I fell back on the bed.

Sterling, why are you letting me down? I have done everything for you. Everything that is mine is to be yours. You and Tricia and I can and will have everything we deserve. It is my mission, and I will complete it. You need to listen to your mother.

I stood back up with renewed conviction. Sterling had always worked so hard to please me. He would be devastated if he ever felt I was disappointed or that he let me down.

I made my way to the barn. I found the horse rope coiled up along the back wall. I took the one end and loosely fashioned the fatal knot.

Oh, Lord, Sterling, please don't make this necessary.

I dropped the rope on the porch, gathered my thoughts, and entered the front door of the guesthouse.

Sterling looked up from the rodeo that was playing on the television and glared at me. "What do you want, Mom?"

"Honey, please calm down. We need to finish our talk. We need to be rational. I love you, son."

"I love you too, Mom. I would do anything for you. You know that. But lately, you have been acting strange."

I went to the kitchen and grabbed two beers. I turned off the TV as I joined Sterling on the couch, handing him a beer. "Honey, there is something you need to know. Something I just found out myself."

He looked at me quizzically and took a drink of his beer. "What is it?"

"Sterling, Jasper and Tricia are half siblings. Tricia's father had an affair with Jasper's mother."

Sterling's jaw dropped to the floor. "Oh my god!" was all he could say at first. Then, eventually, he said, "Does Trish know?"

"Why do you think she is in that hospital?" I answered.

"You told me it was because of the fighting with Jasper," he responded animatedly, throwing his arms in the air.

"I am sorry. I should have told you."

"Jasper? Does Jasper know?"

"No, Sterling. Jasper doesn't know, and we can't tell him."

"What the heck are you talking about, Mom? Obviously, we have to tell Jasper. We have to tell him right now!" He reached for his cell phone. "What will he—" he continued.

"Sterling, please stop," I interrupted and begged in a soft and loving tone as I took the phone from him. "Don't you understand? Jasper will take everything. He will take the Merwood fortune from us. But more than that, he is a Maxwell. He will try to take this farm from us. Our farm, Sterling."

Sterling began pacing the floor and waving his arms around hysterically.

"What are you talking about, MOTHER? The 'Merwood fortune' isn't ours in the first place. This is crazy talk. This is what I am talking about. This is how you have been acting…"

I was losing him. But I had to keep going.

"Sterling, please, please understand. We need to kill Jasper. Please…"

"Oh my god! Mom? Kill Jasper? Who are you? First, you killed Emma, and don't dare try to tell me you didn't, and now you want to kill Jasper! I need to put **you** in that hospital."

I could not stop the tears that began to flow.

"Sterling, my son, it is the only way. Please don't disappoint me. Please listen to your mother."

"You are not my mother! I don't know who you are! Do you hear yourself? This is insane! Absolutely insane!" He turned his back to me and paced to the far wall.

I felt the tears welling up.

Sterling, you've left me no choice.

I dropped the full contents of the vial into Sterling's beer.

After a deep breath, I started, "Okay, son, I know you are right. I am sorry. Please calm down. We will tell Jasper. Please come sit with me. Let's talk this through." I offered him his beer.

"Mom, what were you thinking?" Sterling pleaded as he took the bottle from me.

I watched as he drained the remaining contents.

"Honey, I was just thinking about us. You know how much I love you…" With that, I could no longer speak. I headed out the front door.

"I love you too, Mom. Where are you…" was all I heard from Sterling behind me as I exited.

When I returned with the rope, Sterling was sitting on the edge of the coffee table, his elbows on his knees. He slumped to the rug.

"Mom, I don't feel well."

"I know, sweetie. I know. I poisoned your beer. You understand why." I came close. Sterling looked at me and then at the rope, and he knew. A solitary tear rolled down his cheek.

I climbed the stairs to the loft. I looked down at Sterling and tossed one end of the rope over the exposed crossbeam so that the noose was about seven feet off the floor just in front of him. I tied the other end tightly to the banister. Returning to Sterling, I wrapped my arms around my son and hugged him tight. He was limp.

Looking into his eyes, I told Sterling I forgave him. He just stared at me.

I helped him to his feet and pulled the coffee table forward, positioning it properly under the noose. I climbed onto the table first. With my hands under his arms, I pulled him up to me.

I placed the noose around his neck. He did not fight it.

My beautiful boy.

Sterling's breathing was shallow by this point from the drug. I hugged him tight again, kissed him on the forehead, and thanked him for being the best son a mother could ask for. I kissed him good-bye and then pushed the table from underneath his feet back toward the couch.

I heard his garbled gasps behind me but could not bear to turn around.

I fell to the floor. The grief was overwhelming, but I had to keep going. I went to Sterling's laptop and typed the note that he would have written:

> **Dear Mom,**
>
> **We may not share the same blood, but you are my mother. I have felt your love and devotion from my earliest memories. You have always been so kind to me...given me so many opportunities.**
>
> **I have disappointed you. Please forgive me.**
>
> **Love,**
> **Your Sterling**

CHAPTER 40

December 23, 2018, 12:30 AM

The shower was intended to clean my hands and my mind. It did neither.

What have I done? What have I done? I have done nothing. Jasper, you did this, and you will pay for it.

I slipped on my heavy riding pants and black thermal shirt. My hair was wrapped neatly in a bun. I started to pull on my riding boots, but then I thought better of it. No, there was a better way of handling this. For now, the jogging shoes will do.

I ran back down to the guesthouse.

Sorry to disturb you, my dear Sterling. You gave me the brilliant idea earlier, and I must see it through.

Sterling's oversize muck boots were perfect for the job ahead. As were his work coat and ski cap. In addition, I required some gloves. I grabbed a thin knit pair from the house and then found a latex set in the barn.

It was cold, but at least, there was no snow on the ground yet to worry about tracks.

This plan will work. It has to work.

*****

It was about 1:15 AM when I drove past the Oak Barrel Bed and Breakfast. I noticed a light on in one of the guest rooms, so I circled the block and drove past in the opposite direction. There was a parking lot with hedges diagonal from the B&B. This presented as the perfect cover. I took another trip around the block and then pulled into that lot, hiding Sterling's truck behind the hedges.

Come on, people! Just go to sleep!

*****

At last I watched the final light go out. After waiting another thirty minutes to make sure everyone was asleep, I was ready to make my move. I pulled the crowbar from the bed of Sterling's truck and checked my pocket for the utility knife and flashlight.

Time to get this done once and for all.

I made my way to the back of the B&B and found an old casement window. Using the crowbar, I slowly jimmied it open without making more than a slight cracking sound, making sure not to leave any marks. I pulled the pane outward and shined the light into what appeared to be an old storage closet.

Perfect.

I shimmied feet first through the window and dropped the final foot to the floor with ease. My light found the door, and I carefully opened it just enough to squeeze my body through. Now to find the furnace room.

This wasn't hard because I could hear the hum of the running motor. Although Harry Broadmoar kept the old house in great condition and was very handy, thankfully, the furnace was quite old. I cut through the tape that joined the flue pipes together and pulled them slightly apart until I saw a gap on the back side. Next, I pulled the air filter from its slot and used the utility knife to loosen the fiberglass, causing it to bunch up, before sliding it back into place.

Better to be safe than sorry. I can't afford this not to work.

I moved the switch on the furnace to "Continuous" to ensure the furnace would keep running despite the temperature set on the gauge upstairs.

I looked around for any signs of a carbon monoxide detector and found none.

Getting out of the window proved a little more difficult, but thankfully, I was in good shape. I jumped and grabbed ahold of some pipes that were jointed near the window and kicked my legs through the window. Keeping as much weight on my feet as possible, I walked my hands along the pipes closer and closer to the window until I was able to shift my hips on the ground and push myself all the way out.

My hat caught on a piece of jagged wood of the window frame, but fortunately, I caught it before it fell back into the basement. *Whew!*

I pushed the window back in place and used my elbow to give it one good shove to secure it. I ran my gloved hands around the perimeter and could not detect any misalignment that would catch someone's eye. Next, I spread the leftover fall leaves around the area to cover my boot marks. As I stood there, I shined the light all around and was satisfied that no one would notice this area had been used to break in. Hopefully, the forecasted snow would start soon and provide an additional layer of cover.

My heart was pounding as I put my hat back on. I had one more thing to do before heading back to the truck. Despite my intention of sending carbon monoxide throughout the house to kill Jasper and Mary, I hoped to spare Harry and Susan Broadmoar. They were such a sweet couple, and I would hate to see them end up as collateral damage.

I went around to the back of the house to what I knew was the master bedroom. The room had two large windows, but unfortunately, I was unable to budge either one. I tried the back door, but it was also locked. Thankfully, the small window above the kitchen sink lifted when I gave it a push. As I backed away, I took a last look.

I hoped that window would provide enough fresh air to give Harry and Susan a fighting chance.

*****

Taking a deep breath, I entered the guesthouse for the fourth time tonight.

If only you could have seen things my way, Sterling. If only...

I replaced the boots and the keys and made sure nothing looked suspicious. I took one last sad glance at Sterling and blew him a kiss goodbye as I backed out and locked the guesthouse door. The walk up the hill seemed to take forever. It had been a long day. As I reached the house, the snow began to fall in earnest.

*****

Surprisingly, sleep came easily and quickly. I awoke just before seven and called Jasper's cell immediately. I hoped for no answer or maybe a solemn police officer giving me the news I expected.

"Cheryl," Jasper answered.

No, no, no! How could this be? How many lives do you have, Jasper Merwood?

CHAPTER 41

Present Time

A text from Jasper broke Cheryl from her thoughts. It stated that Jasper and Tricia were on their way. It would be just the two of them. Mary was going to be over at the Oak Barrel Bed and Breakfast assisting with the investigation. Cheryl wasn't concerned with that. She was relieved that Mary would not be at dinner and happily removed one setting from the table. She was also happy Tricia would be coming home from the hospital, even if it was not how she planned it earlier this morning.

CHAPTER 42

December 23, 2018, 10:30 AM

"Wait, what do you mean she can't be discharged until this afternoon?" I was in no mood for this conversation or for the delay.

"She needs to be seen by her attending physician before we can let her go, and Dr. Alexander won't be making his rounds for another couple of hours," the nurse at the desk explained.

I could not hide my frustration and demanded that I speak with somebody else…somebody in charge. The nurse gave me a dirty look and picked up the phone. She explained to the person on the other end that a very upset visitor would like to speak to Margie as soon as possible. She nodded then hung up.

"Mrs. Maxwell, the nursing supervisor will get here when she can."

It was clearly going to be a while, so I wandered over to the little kitchen area nearby and poured myself a coffee. I took a seat at the small table along the wall.

So many thoughts flooded my head. I had to try to sort it all out and determine where to go from here. Jasper was alive. Sterling was dead. Police were probably all over the guesthouse. Police are at the Broadmoars. Everybody was looking for Tricia.

What a mess.

Jasper. I need to take care of Jasper. How is he still alive? How many times is he going to slip away? I just need to finish him off once and for all. And that PI Mary too!

I needed to get Tricia home and break the awful news about Sterling. I headed back to the nurses' station and demanded to take Trish home now. Again, I was rebuffed.

The nurse chided me like I was a child, "Now, we wouldn't want your daughter to go home before she is ready. We wouldn't want her to hurt herself, now, would we?"

I slammed my fist on the desk, and in a raised voice, I explained, "I know what is best for my daughter! I am going back to get her and take her home whether Margie says it's okay or not."

With that, the guard at the nearby security desk jumped up and asked if there was a problem. The startled nurse explained the situation, and the guard asked me to join him at the desk.

I silently cursed myself as I walked over with the nurse in tow. It was my thoughts of Jasper that had gotten the better of me. Jasper always had a way of riling me up.

"Cheryl? Cheryl! What are you doing here? Do you know that Tricia is here?"

Jasper? I nearly jumped out of my skin. *How did he find me?*

"Jasper, Mary?" *Calm down, Cheryl. Officer Jancy? What the... deep breath.* "Yes, Jasper, Tricia is here, and she doesn't want to see you."

My mind was racing. *What does this all mean? What do they know?* Jasper was in a tirade, and my nurse nemesis standing beside me hushed him up.

"Why is Tricia here, and why doesn't she want to see me?" Jasper questioned.

"Jasper, you are the reason she is here. You put her here, and now, you need to leave us alone." *If only that was humanly possible.*

"She is my wife! You have lied to me for days! You knew how worried I have been, yet you lied to me! Sterling lied to me. I sat around your breakfast table this morning, and I feared my wife was dead, and you said nothing. Nothing! How could you? You probably also knew Sterling was dead, yet you let me find him like that!" Jasper announcing Sterling's death out loud had a numbing effect on me. Sort of made it all more real.

I forced surprise. "Sterling is dead? What are you talking about, Jasper? What do you mean Sterling is dead? What did you do to Sterling?"

Mary stepped in to calm things down.

Whatever.

After a bit, it was clear there was nothing I could do to stop Jasper from seeing Tricia. My rage at Jasper and my heightened awareness of Sterling's death had left me in tears. I needed to get home and regroup.

"Fine, Jasper. Go. You win this round, but this fight isn't over. Not by a long shot!"

I went back to UBB, poured myself a glass of bourbon, and sat down in silence in front of the unlit fireplace. The events at the hospital this morning had not gone as planned. None of the last few days had gone as planned.

CHAPTER 43

Present Time

Jasper and Tricia arrived at the farm and burst through the front door.

"Cheryl? Mom?" they called out. The wonderful smells of the dinner drew them to the kitchen. There they found Cheryl sitting at the table set for three.

"Tricia, Jasper, let's talk…"

CHAPTER 44

December 27, 2018, 9:30 AM

Jasper, Tricia, and Cheryl sat in silence for a while at the kitchen table of the farmhouse. The eggs and coffee that sat in front of them had long ago gone cold. The past four days had hit them all like a ton of bricks, and they were exhausted. Sterling's funeral had been a solemn affair, and the weather matched the occasion. The dreary, steady, cold rain blew in alternating directions and made sure each and every person at the burial services was as uncomfortable as possible.

With those services over, Jasper and Tricia now faced their uncertain future head-on. Eventually, Jasper broke the silence.

"Well, I better call my Uber. My flight is at twelve fifteen, and we will need to take our time on the interstate. The weatherman said it is quite icy in spots."

"How long are you going to be in Atlanta?" Tricia inquired.

"I meet with the tax attorneys on Monday morning, and then, I head straight to the airport. I should be home, uh, back in Manhattan, by early evening," Jasper replied.

"I'm going to take off too. I know it's the holiday week, but I'd still like to make the city before the evening rush." Tricia worked through the timing in her mind.

Cheryl asked, "Jasper, do you know when I should expect Mary to pick up your car?"

Jasper recalled his conversation with Mary at the funeral.

"I believe she said she would be by sometime tomorrow."

As Jasper got up from the table, he turned and looked back to Cheryl.

"Do you mind if I take those letters with me? There may be a time, down the road, that I feel like reading about my...my parents."

"No concerns from me. I just threw those disgusting things into one of the desk drawers in the den. I certainly don't need to read any more."

Tricia gave her mother a sad, understanding glance, then she got up and gave Jasper an equally sad hug.

"I will see you Monday," she said before heading upstairs to pack.

PART 3

CHAPTER 45

December 31, 2018, 9:00 PM

Jasper Merwood walked into the Manhattan condo, exhausted from the events of this past week. Tricia had been anticipating his return. Due to the circumstances at hand, instead of partaking in the traditional New York City New Year's Eve festivities, they sat on the sofa, staring at the unopened presents under the unlit Christmas tree.

CHAPTER 46

December 31, 2018, 9:00 PM

Officer Curtis Jancy and Mary Sintag had been busy investigating both the Sterling suicide and the furnace malfunction at the Broadmoars' Oak Barrel Bed and Breakfast. Things didn't add up almost instantly for Mary, and her instincts proved correct yet again. This New Year's Eve evening, instead of patrolling the area for drunk drivers, Officer Jancy was knocking on the front door of the farmhouse with an arrest warrant for Cheryl Maxwell in his hand.

CHAPTER 47

December 31, 2018, 9:00 PM

"Arrival time at JFK International Airport is 10:25 PM. Enjoy your flight and Happy New Year," the pilot announced over the intercom system.

Cheryl looked out the window of the 737.

Happy New Year, Jasper. See you soon.

CHAPTER 48

December 31, 2018, 9:05 PM

"Jancy, what's wrong?"

"How did you know something was wrong, Mary?"

"Why else would you be calling me when you are supposed to be arresting Cheryl Maxwell?"

"Well, yeah, about that. Cheryl isn't here. No answer at the door. Car is not in the garage."

"Can you get a search warrant? We need to make sure she didn't skip town with the evidence."

"I'm sure I can. Judge JT Wright is on duty tonight and owes me a favor. Why do you think she skipped town? How would she know we were on to her? We've been hush-hush about this investigation all week."

"Jancy, nothing about Cheryl surprises me anymore. We need to get in that house!"

"WE?"

"Yes, WE," answered Mary emphatically. "I'll meet you at the farmhouse in an hour."

CHAPTER 49

December 31, 2018, 9:05 PM

Jasper picked up the envelope containing the letters from his mother Paige to his "father" Rex. "Are you sure you want to read those?" Tricia asked.

"I wasn't ready before, but here with you now, I think I am. Everything we've had, everything we were building, is crushed. I know your mom explained the affair started at Uncle Phillip's wedding, but why didn't Paige and Rex ever get together? Is there something in these letters that could explain more than your mom told us?"

"Oh, Jasper, my mind has been spinning all week. I am creeped out by the fact that I am married to my brother—even though you are a great guy." Trish forced a smile at Jasper. "I just want our attorney to call to say the annulment has been approved. I've enlisted a real estate agent to find me a new apartment. Nothing promising yet, but it's kind of tough around the holidays, I guess. Anyway, we need to figure out where we go from here."

Jasper took Tricia's hand.

"I've been giving the future a lot of thought while in Atlanta." Noticing some packing boxes in the corner of the living room, Jasper

177

turned toward Tricia and continued, "Hear me out, Trish. I know I've been a jerk lately. But when I didn't know where you were, I went nuts. I determined to be a better hus—um…a better person to you. There is no doubt that you and I felt an extreme connection from the moment we met. We have shared some great times together. I want more. There's no reason that just because we can't be husband and wife, that our lives need to change all that dramatically."

"What are you suggesting, Jasper?"

"I am suggesting that you unpack those boxes, and we continue to live here together, differently, but together, at least for now. Let me share your joys of journalism, cooking, and biking. You can help me spend my millions once Edward's estate is settled." Jasper raised his eyebrows inquisitively in an attempt to entice Trish to consider his proposal.

"Jasper, are you still entitled to Edward's fortune if you are not really his son?"

"Yep! I talked with our attorneys in Atlanta. The will names me as an heir, and since Emma is gone, after probate, I'll also get her portion. There is nothing about me needing to be his biological son. It's all mine, Trish."

The two of them sat in silence, staring at the New Year's Eve coverage on the TV.

Finally, Jasper spoke again, "But for now, we need to read these letters and try to figure out what our parents were thinking."

"You're right. I'll pour us a drink. You start reading."

It was obvious that Cheryl had haphazardly put the letters in the manila envelope as the postmarks were out of order. There were thirty total spanning one and a half years. He put them in chronological order and opened the first one dated October 15, 1990, as Tricia returned with the drinks.

"Here goes nothing," Jasper said as he exhaled deeply then took a gulp of alcohol.

> My Dearest Rex,
> Words cannot describe how I am feeling right now. My time with you at UBB was the

most alive I have felt in I don't know how long. The way you and I connected was amazing. I keep thinking about our walks and time spent in the winery showroom, talking about everything under the sun. I miss you so much already, and it's only been a few days since my brother's wedding. I wish I could rewind time and never say goodbye. I am looking forward to our trip to Spain next month. I love Pamplona. It's one of the most romantic places on earth. Please write when you can.

Yours,
Paige

Cheryl had already given them a synopsis of the affair that resulted in Jasper. Tricia was not as curious about the letters as he was, but she wanted to support him in his need to know more.

"Well, that was short and sweet. Next?" was all Tricia felt like saying.

Jasper carefully folded the first letter and returned it to the envelope. Jasper opened the next several letters and read them to Tricia. All were pretty much the same: "I love you," "I miss you," and "I can't wait to see you again."

"Well, one thing is for certain, Trish. Rex and Paige were in love."

"These letters are very romantic actually. Let me take over for a little while." The next one on the pile was postmarked September 15, 1991:

Thank you for the beautiful letter, my love.

I miss you, and I can't wait to be together again. I have cleared my schedule to be able to join you at the Napa Valley Harvest Festival next week. I can't believe it's been almost two months since we were together last. I know that between my Hollywood schedule and your domineering wife, we can't be together as much as we'd like.

179

But I want you to know that I cannot wait to be in your arms again.

Yours,
Paige

"'Domineering wife.' Yeah, I can see that. Mom is controlling. I can understand why my dad needed an escape, but why do you think your mom fell in love with him? I mean, your dad…um…Edward… was rich and handsome and pretty much let her have her career. Why start a love affair with someone else if she didn't really have time for the relationship she had?"

"I don't know, Trish. Maybe it was because he was too busy making millions to pay attention to my mom's career? Even when they were together, he had no interest in talking about her movies. I remember one time over-hearing them argue about how he wouldn't attend the Oscars award ceremony when she was nominated for one of her films. Everyone wants attention and to feel special. I guess Rex gave that to her."

"I get it, Jasper. I guess I'm just saying that at the time of their affair, she and Edward had only been married a short time, right? If it wasn't working, why not just get a divorce?"

"Like you said, he was rich." Jasper finished the rest of his vodka tonic and went for a refill. Tricia picked up another letter and started reading loud enough for Jasper to hear in the other room:

January 20, 1992

Rex, Darling,

I have some wonderful news! I am sorry you have to hear this in a letter, but I don't dare take the chance of calling you in case Cheryl is around. Our wonderful rendezvous just before Christmas has yielded a late present. I am pregnant! I know this complicates everything. For one, my director is going to have a lot of creative filming to sched-ule with this unplanned change in my figure. But

seriously, it is time to tell Cheryl and Edward. It
is time for us to be a family! I cannot wait to see
you again in person to celebrate our new life!

> Yours,
> Paige

"Trish? Wait a minute. Let me see that." Jasper practically spilled his drink as he reached for the letter. "Trish!"

"What, Jasper? What is it?" said Tricia, shocked by Jasper's reaction.

"Look at the date on this letter. January 1992. I was born in February 1993. Unless my mother had the longest pregnancy in history, this letter is not referring to me!"

They stared at each other.

"Jasper, do you know what this means?"

"I know exactly what it means. Your crazy mother jumped to conclusions without paying attention to the details and put us through turmoil for nothing. Rex isn't my father. We aren't siblings. Trish, you are not my sister!"

They both jumped to their feet and embraced. Tricia was bouncing up and down as Jasper was holding her tight.

"We're not related!" More embracing.

"But wait, Jasper," Tricia said as she pulled away. "There's still more letters. We need to finish them to be sure."

Hearts pounding, each of them picked up another letter and started skimming through the words. Tricia was the first to share what she was reading:

February 24, 1992

Rex, my dearest Rex,

It is with deepest regrets that I write you
today. I hate to even put this news on paper, but
my doctor has just informed me that our beautiful child is no more. There is nothing more I can

add to this note. Please call me whenever you can find a safe moment to do so.

So sorry,
Paige

Jasper and Tricia looked at each other. Their initial reaction was sympathy for the pregnancy loss, but surges of relief and joy took back over in full swing.

"Mine is just as sad," said Jasper.

April 7, 1992

Rex,

It has been a year and a half, and you have yet to leave Cheryl. I can't continue waiting for this much longer. I won't. Rex, it is now or never…

Paige

Tricia had already started on her next letter while Jasper finished.

May 3, 1992

Rex,

I am sorry for Cheryl and her accident. I am. But c'mon, it is just a horse at the end of the day, but I understand how hard this is for you right now. You have that little girl to take care of. You are needed there, Rex, and you aren't going to leave. That is clearer now than ever before. I don't hold this against you. We met too late.

Yours,
Paige

Tricia wiped a tear from her eye. The emotion was not driven from the seeming end of the Rex-and-Paige love story. Oddly, the emotion was for her mother. Tricia placed herself in her mother's shoes for a moment. Cheryl's life had been destroyed so many years ago. She had heard about how devastated her mother was after Snow died. Roger had told her more than once that her mother became a different person after that.

No wonder Mom had acted so irrationally the last couple of weeks. How awful to find out that the toughest time of your life is made worse by finding out your husband was having an affair the whole time.

Jasper broke Tricia's thoughts by announcing he was reading the last letter:

June 23, 1992

Rex,

     I thought you might want to know. I am pregnant. It is Edward's.... Goodbye, Rex.

                                    Paige

"So there you have it, Trish. No doubt that I am Edward Merwood's son." He smiled at his beautiful wife who was smiling back at him. She leaned in; Jasper gently cupped her face in his hands, and they kissed. All the sadness, fear, and uncertainty had been lifted.

Tossing the letters off the couch, they made love like never before.

*****

"I am hungry. How about a snack?"

"I just had dessert." Jasper winked. "But, yes, I could eat something."

Tricia smiled. "I will throw a cheese and cracker tray together. Let's drink some wine, watch the ball drop, and then open those Christmas presents. What do you think?'

"I think that is a fabulous idea, my beautiful wife!" Jasper exclaimed, emphasizing the "wife." "I'll grab a shower."

Tricia headed for the kitchen. She put a bottle of UBB strawberry wine in the ice bucket and placed the tray with wineglasses on the coffee table. In the kitchen, she cut up some cheese and piled it in the center of the tray. She ringed the outside of the tray with crackers. She could hear the shower was still running. She looked at the clock: 11:30 PM. It was New Year's Eve. Mom will probably still be up. She started to dial.

CHAPTER 50

December 31, 2018, 11:00 PM

Mary had been waiting at the farmhouse for Officer Curtis Jancy to return with the search warrant. It was a frigid winter night, yet Mary was outside, bundled in her parka and boots, hands in her pockets, pacing the front porch. It seemed like an eternity since the first time she walked up these steps, hopeful that Trish would greet her at the door. A little more than a week ago, it had looked so beautiful and peaceful; now, it seemed dark and evil.

The investigation into the furnace malfunction at the Broadmoars and Sterling's suicide had been exhausting these past eight days. But she was motivated from both gut instinct and friendship not to give in to simple explanations. She knew Sterling wouldn't kill himself, and she was bound to prove it.

Her police and private investigation training were formal teachings in processes that came intuitively to Mary. Even when she doesn't realize she's doing it, she was soaking up minor details that would be recalled later. And that's exactly what happened at the guesthouse the day she and Jasper found Sterling.

*****

There was something about the proximity of Sterling's hanging body to the only piece of furniture close enough for him to have stood on before taking a leap to his death: the coffee table. That "something" turned out to be important evidence. When Officer Jancy phoned the policeman on duty to treat the guesthouse like a crime scene, the thorough forensics team did their job well.

Cheryl's fingerprints were on the beer bottle, but that could only prove she had a drink in the guesthouse, not that she killed Sterling. Her fingerprints were also on the laptop keyboard. That only proves that she used the computer, not that she typed the suicide letter. But the fact that her fingerprints were found *under* the top of the coffee table showed that she had at some point pulled the table, leaving her fingerprints under and her thumbprint on top.

Another thing about that coffee table proved important: the crime-scene photographs showed slide marks on the rug…as if the table had been moved twice. The last time it was moved, it was not returned to the original location because the divot marks were visible.

It is plausible that the table could have moved slightly when Sterling jumped after placing the noose around his neck, but why would there be marks showing it had been slid out and back? Because it wasn't moved by Sterling; it was moved by Cheryl.

Mary knew these details were not enough to convince anyone else that Cheryl murdered her friend. She remained patient for the toxicology reports to come back. And there it was: a high level of barbiturates was found in Sterling's blood. There was no evidence of where it came from, not on his person, in the house, or in his truck. The pathologist said the drug at this level would have killed him within minutes. Why take enough drugs to kill oneself and then still go through the trouble of hanging—all within a few minutes? One wouldn't.

She looked at her watch. Jancy was already nearly an hour late. Mary ignored the officer in the heated police car. She was recalling visions of Sterling hanging in the guesthouse and then again lying lifeless and artificial in the casket at the funeral home.

We'll get her, Sterling.

*****

It was nothing less than true fate that Mary met Chloe Broadmoar at the funeral services for Harry and Susan. The police found no evidence of foul play at the Oak Barrel Bed and Breakfast and had ruled their deaths accidental. Mary's senses were strong that the furnace malfunction was no accident, and she gave Chloe her business card and asked her to call if she found anything out of the ordinary.

Earlier this morning, Mary received a phone call from Chloe. It turned out that as she was going through her parents' belongings, she found an app on their computer for an online service that recorded motion-detected activity from the camera positioned on the garage at the end of the B&B's driveway. Even she didn't know her father had installed this camera. She was shocked to see a dark figure moving around the house the night of the incident. Chloe pulled Mary's business card from her purse and called to report what she found.

The police were able to enhance the video and saw Cheryl Maxwell putting a ski cap on as she walked from the side to the back of the house. It showed her attempting to open the back door and then successfully opening the window in the kitchen before leaving the sight line of the camera.

Mary knew this wasn't an attempt to kill the Broadmoar couple; this was an attempt to keep her and Jasper from finding Tricia. Cheryl murdered the Broadmoars with the hopes of killing her and Jasper.

*****

Officer Jancy showed up with two more police cars, sirens blaring, lights flashing.

187

"What took you so long?"

"All that matters is that I got the warrant," Jancy said as he skipped up the steps to the porch, waving the papers in his hand. Two of the officers behind him were carrying the battering ram that would be used to open the locked door.

Mary stepped aside.

"Okay, let's do this."

Moments later, they entered the farmhouse and began to spread out. Mary headed to the den.

Jancy barked, "Remember, we are looking for anything suspicious that can connect Ms. Maxwell to the murder. Myers and Bridge, you take upstairs. Garmen, you're with me down here."

After a few moments, Officer Myers yelled down. "Hey, Jance, I think our suspect is on the move. I have an empty suitcase sitting on the bed."

Jancy went back to find Mary to give her that news and found her at the desk digging through the doors.

Just then, Mary shouted, "Bingo!"

"What do you have?" Jancy asked.

"The password for the computer. Oh, I forgot, you guys haven't moved into the twentieth century yet, let alone the twenty-first down at that police station of yours." She looked up and gave Jancy a playful wink. "Anyway, nowadays, they make you create passwords for everything, and each site has their own validation rules, so everybody has to write them down and leave them near the computer. Really kind of defeats the purpose. Anyway, here it is, Sn0w4Gold."

"I'll have you know I am quite the computer whiz at home. In fact, many of my friends think I should do side work for the geek squad." He playfully slapped her on the shoulder.

"Friends? You have friends?" Mary acted surprised and laughed.

"Anyway," Jancy told her about the suitcase as Mary entered the password.

Mary then announced, "Well, that makes sense. Check this out."

On the screen, Cheryl was still logged in to the United Airlines website, and the itinerary showed she had landed in New York City less than an hour ago.

Jancy looked over Mary's shoulder and commented, "What would she be doing there? Do you think she went to visit Tricia?"

Mary clicked the back arrow to return to the e-mail screen. After a few clicks, she whispered under her breath, "Oh my god! She pushed Jasper in front of that train!"

"What are you talking about?" Jancy looked at her in shock.

"Her trip on the twenty-first. Cheryl strategically left out that her 'business trip' was in New York City. This confirmation says that a round-trip ticket was purchased that morning. It wasn't a planned trip as she played it up to be. It was spur-of-the-moment."

"Meetings can pop up at the last minute, Mary. But you just said she pushed Jasper in front of a train. What are you talking about?"

"That's the night that Jasper called me about Tricia. He told me how he nearly fell in front of an oncoming train, but luckily, someone pulled him to safety before getting flattened. He said he was certain he was pushed. I'll tell you what, Curtis, I don't like that Cheryl is in New York City right now…especially after what she did at the Broadmoars."

Suddenly, Officer Myers came running in. "I think you two are going to want to see this."

She led Mary and Jancy upstairs to the dressing room. A box containing two vials marked as sodium pentobarbital sat on the counter. It was clear by the empty spaces that there used to be more.

"I think Cheryl is a serial killer." Mary's statement seemed to hover in the air.

"I'll fill you in later, but I believe that after more investigation, we can not only tie Cheryl to Sterling's murder, but also to Jasper's father. This may be the mysterious drug that police in Atlanta are looking for."

With no time to waste, Mary continued, "Jasper and Tricia are in danger. I need to call them now. I'm afraid Cheryl is on her way to kill Jasper!" She looked at the clock. 11:30 PM. Cheryl had been on the ground for over an hour. She pulled out her cell phone and began to dial Tricia.

Before Mary could send the call, the farmhouse phone rang. Mary and Jancy raced back down the stairs and into the den. After four rings, the answering machine clicked on, and after the beep, they heard Tricia.

"Hey, Mom, are you there? Okay, well, I guess you must have big plans this New Year's Eve. Jasper and I have some big news as well—"

Mary picked up.

CHAPTER 51

December 31, 2018, 11:30 PM

Trish looked at the clock as her mother's voice began to speak to her from the answering machine. She had previously called her mother's cell but was unsuccessful. Either Cheryl had shut down 2018 early, or she was out ringing in the New Year in style. Either way, Trish was disappointed that she would have to wait to relay her and Jasper's news.

Beep. "Hey, Mom, are you there?" Tricia paused a moment before continuing. "Okay, well, I guess you must have big plans this New Year's Eve. Jasper and I have some big news as well—"

"Tricia, hold on! It's Mary."

"Mary? Hi. What are you doing at the farmhouse? Where's my mom? Is she okay?"

"Well, Trish, that's what we are wondering."

"Who is we?" she stuttered, confused.

"Officer Jancy, his team, and me. Trish, I have so much I need to catch you up on. Are you sitting down?" Mary asked.

"Officer Jancy? Mary, what in the world is going on? Is my mother okay? Please let me talk to her!" Trish's voice rose and conveyed concern and impatience.

"Tricia. Listen. I am here with the police. Your mother is not here. We have a search warrant."

"A search warrant? Why in heaven's sake would you need a—"

"Tricia. Listen!" Mary interrupted. "We have a warrant for your mother's arrest for the murders of Harry and Susan Broadmoar."

"Oh my god! What! Mary, my mother is a lot of things, but she is not a murderer! Seriously? I can't believe you would even say such a thing! I called to tell my mom the wonderful news that Jasper is not my half brother, and you try to ruin it with all this crap!"

"Jasper is not your brother? That is wonderful!" Mary started.

There was a knock at Tricia's door. "Hold on, Mary. Someone is here. Who the heck could that be this late?"

Tricia opened the door and saw Cheryl.

"Mom, what are you doing here? I just tried to call you. I am on the phone with—"

Mary quickly screamed into the phone, "Don't tell her it's me!"

"Uh…a friend," Tricia stammered and then gave Cheryl a hug. "I will be just a minute. Go ahead and hang your coat in the closet and have a seat. Can I get you a drink?"

"Certainly, honey. Take your time. A glass of wine would be great. Where's Jasper?" Cheryl asked, more to herself, as Trish had already exited to the kitchen in the rear of the condo.

Trish was very much on edge by her mother's unexpected arrival as well as the unfathomable things Mary was saying and the frightening tone of Mary's voice. "What is going on?" Tricia whispered into the phone to Mary.

"Trish, listen closely to what I am about to tell you. You have to trust me."

She felt sick by the details Mary was spewing at her. "You need to be careful, Trish. We are calling the police. Don't let Jasper drink anything! And don't let Cheryl leave."

Trish was trying hard to hold back tears. She answered Mary with a nod of her head, and then after a moment, realizing her error, she said, "Okay," and she hung up.

Tricia could not believe what she had just heard. She was shaking. She took a moment to compose herself before returning to the living room with a wineglass in hand. Cheryl was sitting in the center of the couch, watching the aged Kool & the Gang finishing up a rendition of "Celebrate." Then, the screen changed, and Carson Daly and Chrissy Teigen, dressed in elegant expensive winter attire, appeared as well as a clock that indicated eleven minutes until 2019.

Tricia placed the glass beside the other two on the tray in front of her mother. Cheryl stood, and the two embraced warmly, "This is such a nice surprise!" she forced.

"Where's Jasper?" Cheryl inquired.

"He's in the shower. I'll tell him to hurry up. I don't want him to miss the ball dropping!"

"Sounds great. I will pour the wine," Cheryl said cheerfully.

As Tricia disappeared around the corner toward the bedrooms, Cheryl grabbed a vial from her purse and emptied it into one of the glasses then filled them all with the wine Tricia had chilling.

A couple of minutes later, Trish and Jasper returned.

"Hi, Cheryl. Missed us already, did you?" Jasper joked as he gave her a quick hug.

"I did. I wanted to see how you two were doing and if maybe I could help with anything. You sound chipper," Cheryl responded, handing Jasper a glass of wine.

Tricia quickly said, "Actually, Mom, can you grab the cheese and cracker tray in the kitchen? We can all toast to new beginnings in 2019 at the stroke of midnight."

She whispered to Jasper as Cheryl headed for the kitchen, "Put these letters away. I don't want to upset her."

Jasper put his glass of wine back on the tray and did as he was asked. He turned to put the manila envelope in the side table drawer when Trish handed him a glass of wine and said, "Be ready when Mom comes back. I think she is in a celebratory mood."

"So are we, my wife. I will never get tired of saying that, 'my wife,'" Jasper playfully joked as he pecked Tricia on the cheek.

Cheryl returned and placed the tray of snacks beside the wine.

"Let's raise our glasses to 2019!"

Trish handed her a glass, and the three of them toasted. Cheryl gulped hers down while keeping an eye on Jasper doing the same.

Jasper began to tell a story about his flight home. "You two would not believe what I saw on the plane this evening…" Jasper was telling Trish and Cheryl a story about his flight from Atlanta to New York. "Apparently, back in coach, a passenger had been permitted to bring aboard his emotional support potbellied pig, and the cute creature had caused quite a bit of excitement."

Cheryl did not hear another word of Jasper's rambling. She was lost in thought. *Did you enjoy your drink, Jasper? You son of a cheater and a whore. You are the reason Sterling is dead. I have hated you from the first day I met you. Well, you won't get a dime from UBB, and I will be free of the Merwoods. You will die. Finally. Here. On this couch! Still yammering away? Are you feeling sleepy yet? Do you need to lie down?*

A thin snarky grin snaked across Cheryl's face.

Tricia also missed most of Jasper's story. She was watching her mother.

Is Mary right about you? Are you capable of doing the things she said? Are you a murderer? No, this can't be happening. But why are you smiling like that? Are you really trying to kill Jasper? Mom, please don't let it be true, please.

CHAPTER 52

January 1, 2019, midnight

On the TV screen, the large disco ball was down, and the excited patrons of Times Square hooted, hollered, and kissed.

At that moment, there was a knock on the door followed by shouts of "POLICE! OPEN UP!"

Startled, Jasper, who was just about to kiss his wife, began to rise up from the couch.

"I got it, dear," Tricia said, placing a firm hand on Jasper's shoulder. She opened the door, and four uniformed officers entered the condo.

"Cheryl Maxwell. You are under arrest for the murders of Harold Broadmoar and Susan Broadmoar as well as suspicion of murder of Sterling Shapiro."

Jasper stood up. "Murder? Officers, I think there has been some mistake."

As Cheryl stood, the lead officer, Officer Shah, spoke, "Ma'am, please place your hands behind your back."

As Cheryl complied, handcuffs were placed on her wrists, and the officer continued, "You have the right to remain silent. You have the right—"

Jasper remained dumbfounded and looked from Tricia to Cheryl and back. "Sir, please. This is not possible. She would never—"

"Officer," Tricia cut Jasper off and handed over her wineglass. "I believe you will want to take this with you. It was meant for my husband."

Jasper stood in shock, his mouth agape.

Cheryl turned and looked back over her shoulder as she was guided from the room. "Tricia? How could you?"

THANK YOU

We'd like to extend a special thank-you to our test readers. Your input and observations were invaluable. *A Bond That Breaks* would never have made it to publishing without your efforts. We hope you enjoy your characters!

In order of book appearance:

Emma Brown, a.k.a. Emma Santo: The young second wife of Edward Merwood. In exchange for you putting up with all the discussions, plot changes, and creative differences night after night between these aspiring authors, we gave "you" a rich husband.

Curtis Brown and Leanne Skrjanc Brown, a.k.a. Officer Curtis Jancy: The Westfield police officer enamored by Mary Sintag. See you in the next book!

Margaret "Peggy" Winschel Brown, a.k.a. Peg Winchester: The matriarch of Maple Oak at Van Buren Point visited by Jasper and Tricia. In other words, your fictional alter ego.

Tina Winschel, a.k.a. Tina Marie: Paige Dawson's assistant who had the night off when Paige was killed. In stark contrast, you still await your night off!

Alexander Richard Winschel, a.k.a. Dr. Richard Alexander: The psychiatric doctor who admitted Tricia into the Westfield Community Hospital. Not a far leap from teaching high school students sometimes.

Chloe Winschel, a.k.a. Chloe Broadmoar: The daughter of Oak Barrel Bed & Breakfast owners. Sorry, we killed Rebecca. Sorry, we killed Edward and Emma. Sorry, we killed Sterling. Sorry, we killed…

ABOUT THE AUTHORS

Josh Winschel

This is Josh's inaugural foray into storytelling. Josh is a medical economist by day and resides in Pittsburgh, Pennsylvania. He enjoys basketball, bowling, and cheering on his beloved University of Pittsburgh Panthers. A divorced father of four wonderful children, Josh splits his time between his family and Terri's rapidly growing brood.

Terri Brown

Little did Terri know when she asked Josh to "tell me a story" in 2017, that it would turn into a collaborative effort creating *A Bond That Breaks*. From her home in Ellwood City, Pennsylvania, Terri works as a medical coding auditor and enjoys spending time with her four children, five grandchildren, and one great-grandchild.

CPSIA information can be obtained
at www.ICGtesting.com
Printed in the USA
BVHW072230291021
620256BV00001B/5

9 781649 522214